P9-DOG-479

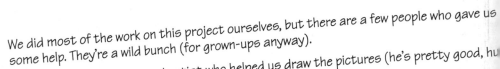

We did most of the work on this project ourselves, but there are a few people who gave us some help. They're a wild bunch (for grown-ups anyway).

Chris Kielesinski is the mad artist who helped us draw the pictures (he's pretty good, hu
Ed van der Maas helped us write the serious stuff.
Rick Osborne helped us put the whole thing together and gave us lots of good ideas.
Terry Van Roon helped us put all the stuff on the pages so they looked good.
Lori Walburg is very good at writing dialogue, so she helped us with that.

Beverly Wiebe and **Randy Arnold** helped us with converting our computer program into
book (it's called DTP); **Tracy Tobin** did the computer colorization; **Mark Herron** took Chr
pencil sketches and added ink to them; and **Lillian Crump** did the "fun maps."

We also want to say "thank you" to **Verlyn Verbrugge**, who wrote some things we used;
Erich J. Elliott and **Shelley Sateren**, who looked through this report before we gave it t
Professor Ed; and a very special thanks to **Stan Gundry**, who believed that we could d

We hope you'll enjoy this report as much as we enjoyed putting it together!

Rebecca

The Adventure Bible Handbook
Copyright © 1994 by Zondervan Publishing House, a Division of the Zondervan Corporation

Cartoon characters (Professor Ed's Kids)
Copyright © 1993 by Zondervan Publishing House and Lightwave Publishing Inc.

If you want to know more about this book, write to Zondervan Publishing House,
Grand Rapids, Michigan 49530 (It's neat – they have their very own zip code!)

Library of Congress Cataloging–in–Publication Data

Van der Maas, Ed M.
    Adventure Bible handbook : a wild and spectacular high–tech trip
through the Bible.
        p.   cm.
    Written by Ed M. van der Maas, illustrated by Chris Kielesinski.
    Includes bibliographical references and index.
    ISBN 0-310-57530-3 (hardcover)
    1. Bible—Juvenile literature. I. Kielesinski, Chris.
    II. Title.
    BS538.V36 1994   93–47210
    220.6'1—dc20   CIP
                                                     AC

Printed in the United States of America

95 96 97 / DW / 9 8 7 6 5 4 3 2

A Lightwave Produc
P.O. Box 160
Maple Ridge, BC, Canada

Tracy's Explanation of Chip's Big Words

(Sometimes Chip makes up words. I think that he made up some of these too!)

Hologram – A hologram can either be a flat picture that looks like it is three-dimensional, or it can be a three-dimensional image, produced by lasers, that seems to float in space. When you are surrounded by holographic images you are in holographic reality, which, of course, really isn't reality at all. (Another name for holographic reality is "virtual reality.")

Holographic image processor – Chip's name for the part of the computer that creates holographic reality.

Infomeld – I don't really understand this either, but it's kind of like putting a bunch of stuff in a blender and making a super-de-luxe milk shake: When Chip puts all the information in the computer and turns it on, all the information is blended together to create holographic reality.

Neuristor skull wires – wires that run from the computer to a helmet; as long as you wear the helmet, you feel like you are inside holographic reality.

Atmospheric blitz – When you wear the helmet with the neuristor skull wires you feel like you are inside holographic reality. When you want to move to a different part of holographic reality (for example, to a different time period), the computer must rearrange its information, and while it is doing that, you sort of feel like you're inside a blender!

Blitz – Same as atmospheric blitz

Multimedia porting – forget it, you don't have to know this one.

Where to Find the Books of the Bible

Some Highlights of Our Adventure

The Garden of Eden

Genesis

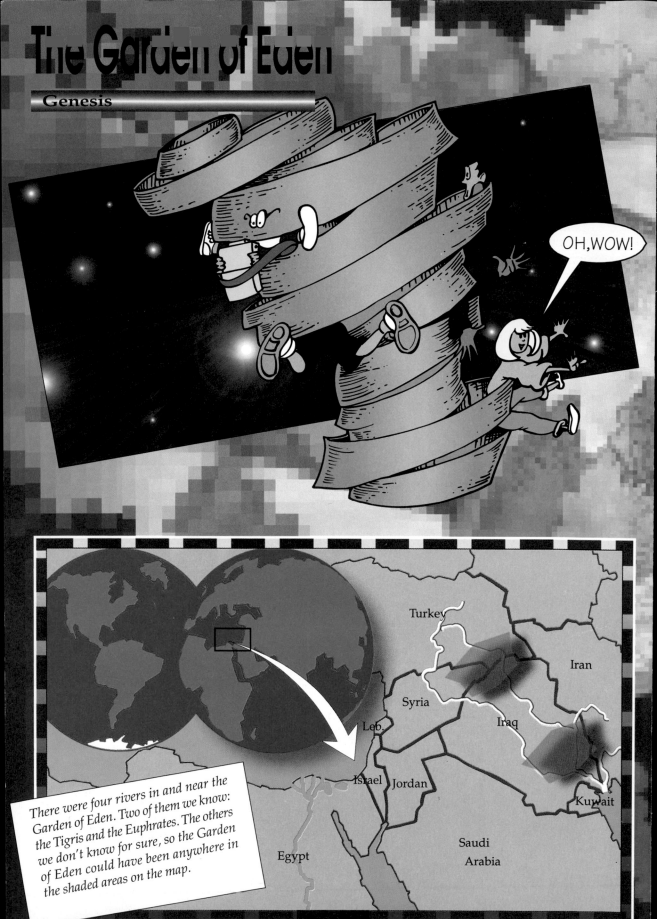

OH, WOW!

There were four rivers in and near the Garden of Eden. Two of them we know: the Tigris and the Euphrates. The others we don't know for sure, so the Garden of Eden could have been anywhere in the shaded areas on the map.

Turkey
Iran
Syria
Iraq
Leb.
Israel   Jordan
Kuwait
Egypt
Saudi Arabia

In the beginning there was nothing: no sound, no light, no people – not even the universe or time or space – only God.

Then God decided to make something marvelous out of nothing. He didn't do anything complicated or wave a magic wand. God simply spoke and everything came into being exactly as he had imagined it.

God created space, the stars and the earth, rain, and trees, and vegetables (even lima beans and brussels sprouts), and lions, and kangaroos, and everything else.

He saved the best for last: When everything was ready, God created two human beings called **Adam and Eve**.

And God was pleased when he saw that Adam and Eve were content (without TV or video games or pizza) because they had everything they could need or want – and most of all because of their friendship with God.

Adam and Eve weren't bored because God put them in charge of the whole Garden of Eden and of all the animals. Life was harmonious and good.
🐸*Genesis 1:1-2:3* 🐸*Genesis 2:4-25*

🐸**Adventure Reading: Psalm 148**

An ancient Babylonian inscription says, "Eridu was a garden, in which was a mysterious sacred tree, a tree of life planted by the gods."

Hey, look! It's Adam and Eve. It looks like they're about to have lunch!

Oh, no!

15

The Fall

G–g–go away! Shoo!

Hold still. Chip will take care of him!

Quit growling you guys – I'm doing the best I can!

click
click
click

But it didn't last. God's enemy, Satan, hates it when things are good and beautiful and people are content. Satan decided that he would try to make Adam and Eve disobey God, because he knew that would destroy the harmony of God's creation and make Adam and Eve and God very unhappy.

So Satan disguised himself as a snake and slithered up a tree – the one tree in the whole Garden of Eden from which Adam and Eve were not supposed to eat – and he waited for Eve to walk by.

Satan convinced Eve to eat from the tree, and Eve talked Adam into doing the same thing (which made Adam the first person to give in to peer pressure!).

So now Adam and Eve had disobeyed God, their Creator and Friend, and they were afraid of God. They hid behind some bushes when God walked through the garden that evening.
Genesis 3:1-24

Effects of Sin on Creation

Adam and Eve's disobedience may seem to be a small thing – just eating a piece of fruit. But that first sin changed the whole creation. Instead of everything working together in harmony, there was disharmony. People now were separated from God and they no longer trusted and loved each other. And the world became a difficult place to live in.

16

What Is Sin?

Sin is doing what God does not want us to do (or sometimes *not* doing what God *does* want us to do). But God didn't make a bunch of rules just to see if we would obey him.

When you get a Nintendo, the people who made it tell you how it should be hooked up and how you should play it. If you ignore those instructions and think you know better, you could blow up your game.

In the same way, God made us and he knows what is best for us – even if we don't understand why we should or should not do something.

We can ignore and disobey him, like Adam and Eve did when they ate from the tree, but we will feel guilty and become afraid of God, just like Adam and Eve.

And if we disobey God often enough, we will get so used to feeling guilty that we won't feel guilty at all any more and we will simply ignore God. That's what a lot of people in the Bible did – and that's what a lot of people do today.

Who Is Satan?

Most Christians believe that Satan (sometimes also called the Devil) was originally an angel created by God. But unlike the other angels, Satan rebelled against God.

Satan's only purpose is to destroy whatever good things God has made. He wants all God's creatures to rebel against God and to sin. (Like Satan, people who rebel against God always try to get others to join them and to sin also: Satan got Eve to sin, and Eve got Adam to sin, and a lot of peer pressure today is an attempt to get people to sin.)

Satan keeps trying and will keep trying to get people to disobey God – even though he has already been defeated because Jesus died on the cross. If you are curious about what will finally happen to Satan, read Revelation 20:10.

Today, a lion and a lamb may lie down together, but the lamb won't get a lot of sleep.

What was that?

Let's get out of here!

PBZZT!!

The Problem

God had said that if Adam and Eve ate from that one tree they would die. And it happened – but not quite as you would expect. Adam and Eve did die eventually and were buried. But as soon as they ate from the tree, they died spiritually.

It was a problem that they themselves could never fix. (It's like when your little brother puts a peanut-butter-and-jelly sandwich in the VCR – you can't fix it; the people who made it will have to fix it.)

Adam and Eve had always done what was right and good – until they disobeyed God. Then they could no longer do only what is right.

Because Adam and Eve had disobeyed God, their friendship with God had been damaged. They now were afraid of God because they knew they had disobeyed him. And there was sadness on God's part.

And it was not just Adam and Eve's problem – it was and is also a problem for all people who lived after them, all their descendants, including you and me!

The Solution

God commanded Adam and Eve to leave the Garden of Eden. He put an angel with a fiery sword at the entrance, so they never could return.

But God still loved them, and he wanted to fix the problem that only he could fix. He didn't want Adam and Eve (or us) to be separated from him forever.

That is why God made a plan to overcome sin and to bring Adam and Eve back to himself.

The result of sin is spiritual as well as physical death. But God doesn't want people to die. He loves us, and that is why he solved the problem by having someone else die in our place: God's own Son, the Lord Jesus.

And so, two thousand years ago, the Son of God came down to earth as a baby in a manger, and he later died on the cross and came back to life. All we have to do is thank God for sending his Son to die for us, and we will once again be God's children.

Our bodies will, of course, still die and be buried, but we will be raised and live forever with God, our Father and our Friend!

You mean we'll see Jesus? I can't wait! Come on, gang- **let's blitz!**

The Flood

Genesis

It's raining cats and dogs!

One of those dumb dogs almost knocked the computer out of my hand!

Adam and Eve had two sons, **Cain and Abel**. Cain didn't like Abel (it is not that unusual for brothers not to get along), so he killed him (which is overdoing it!). That was the first clear result of sin, of Adam and Eve's eating from the forbidden tree. *Genesis 4:1-16*

Later Adam and Eve had many more children. People in those early times lived very long; Adam lived 930 years, and Methuselah, Adam's great-great-great-great-great grandson, lived 969 years!

The world kept getting worse. People did evil and violent things to each other, and finally it got so bad that God decided to get rid of everybody and start over with just one family. God told **Noah** to build a huge boat (the "ark") in his backyard because the greatest flood the world has ever seen was going to wipe out everything and everybody – except Noah and his family and the animals that God sent to Noah. *Genesis 6:5-22*

Stories of the Flood are found in the ancient traditions of the American Indians, of Egypt, Greece, China, India, Mexico, Britain, and other places.

Football Field
360 feet

Boy, this thing sure must have blocked Noah's driveway!

Are you kidding? – it blocked the whole neighborhood!

The flood came with an awesome cloudburst that lasted forty days and forty nights – until even the highest mountains were covered with water.

But Noah and his family and the animals safely floated on top of the waves in the ark. Can you imagine what it must have smelled like inside the ark with all those animals? Finally the water level went down and the ark landed on Mount Ararat – in a silent world without people or animals.

And just as God had made a promise to Adam and Eve that he would make things right between himself and his people, he also made a promise to Noah. God promised that he would never again destroy the world in a flood. The rainbow is, so to speak, God's handshake on that promise.

🐢*Genesis 7:1-24* 🐢*Genesis 8:1-22*
🐢*Genesis 9:8-17*

(Since I'm the artsy one, Brad, Rebecca, Chip, and Jay decided that I should write the stuff for the pictures, so here goes...) This is Mount Ararat with its top in the clouds.

Size of Ark

• *Length: 450 feet*
• *Width: 75 feet*
• *Height: 45 feet*

• *For thousands of years, Noah's ark was the largest ship ever built – until 1858, when the "Great Eastern" was built, which was 669 feet long.*
• *Noah's ark was twice as long as a Boeing 747.*

Noah spent 1 year and 17 days in the ark with his family and the animals.

The Tower Of Babel

Genesis

Many years later, the world was populated again, and all people spoke the same language. One day they got together and came up with what turned out to be a dumb idea: They were going to build a huge city, called Babel, with a tower that would reach to the heavens.

But God put a stop to the plan. The Bible says that God "confused their language." Suddenly they didn't speak the same language any more – which made it hard to ask for a hammer or for a drink! No wonder they couldn't finish their tower. Instead, they broke up into small groups, each with its own language – which was precisely what they had wanted to avoid! 🐸 *Genesis 11:1-9*

Wienershnitzel!

Rigatoni!

Hey, what do you blockheads want to eat? I'm taking orders!

Pommes frites!

Hutspot

Whoa! Look at the size of this thing!

Hey! Down here! Give me two large fries, four double cheeseburgers with everything, and two large shakes…

What are you two babbling about?

In ancient times, gods were worshiped on mountains or "high" places. In places where there were no mountains, people built towers, or ziggurats, to worship on.

The Languages of the Bible

Because of the confusion of languages at Babel, we cannot read the Bible in the languages in which it was originally written.

The Bible was written mostly in two different languages: The Old Testament in Hebrew, and the New Testament in Greek. (A few parts of the Old Testament were written in Aramaic, a language that is a lot like Hebrew.)

To us, Hebrew looks strange. It is written backwards, from right to left, and looks very different from English. Here are the very first words of Genesis in Hebrew:

בְּרֵאשִׁית בָּרָא אֱלֹהִים אֵת הַשָּׁמַיִם וְאֵת הָאָרֶץ

Greek, which in the time of Jesus was the language almost everybody could understand, looks much more like English (some letters are actually the same). Here is the first part of John 3:16 in Greek:

Οὕτως γὰρ ἠγάπησεν ὁ θεὸς τὸν κόσμον, ὥστε τὸν υἱὸν τὸν μονογενῆ

The Bible was written long before paper was invented. The books of the Bible were written on tablets made of clay, or on dried animal skin called parchment, or on sheets of papyrus, made from leaves of the papyrus plant. The parchment or the papyrus pieces were then glued together to form one long strip that was rolled up and called a scroll.

Until printing was invented about five hundred years ago, every copy of the Bible had to be written by hand. In Hebrew and Greek there were originally no spaces between words and only capital letters. If we did that in English it would look like this:

LETMENOTBEP
UTTOSHAMEFO
RITAKEREFUG
EINYOU

(If you can't figure out what this says, read Psalm 25:20.)

What? What did I say wrong? All I said was that the tower was huge!

fineifyouregoin gtotalktomeliketha timnotlistening.

Hombo jumba limbo caramba heeba jeeba mumbo jumbo.*

BLiTN

*Time to blitz our way out of here before none of us make any sense.

23

Abraham

Genesis

The first eleven chapters of the Bible told us how God created a good world that was ruined by sin. Now begins the story of what God did to make everything whole and good again.

It's a long story that takes up the rest of the Bible. It begins with one man, Abraham, a wealthy businessman who lived in the big city of Ur, about a thousand miles due east of Canaan.

One day God told him to leave Ur and to go to the land of Canaan. Abraham listened to God and took his wife, Sarah, and his servants (who also served as armed guards) and all his belongings loaded on camels and donkeys and began the long trip. If you think that Abraham looked forward to the trip, think again! 🌿 *Genesis 12:1-5*

MAX'S GUIDED BIBLE TOURS

SEE THE BIBLE LANDS

Hey, kiddies! Max here! I'm gonna be your tour guide! So what do you wanna see? The tents of Abraham? The pyramids of Egypt? How 'bout a camel ride? Whaddaya say? One hump or two?

Kiddies?!

Psst, Jay. What program did he come from? He's not in the Bible, is he?

Definitely not!

I have never been so insulted in all my life!

I'm not a pet.

People did not need to buy a new camel every few years as we do with cars; a camel lasts forty to fifty years and doesn't need any tune-ups.

Camels Make Lousy Pets

Camels are said to be stupid, very stubborn and malicious. They also have an ugly voice and smell bad. (The South American version of the camel, the llama, even spits.) They make lousy pets, but they are very useful: They can travel as far as 40 miles a day with a load as heavy as 400 pounds, and they can go for several days without water.

Travel

Traveling in Old Testament times wasn't fun – it was dangerous.

We often travel twenty miles or more to go to church, to go shopping, or just to do something fun. But for people who lived in Old Testament times twenty miles was a whole day's trip – one way!

There were no paved roads. Even "interstate highways" were little more than trails from which rocks and trees had been removed. They were clogged by mud after winter rains and dusty and rutted in the hot summertime.

When ancient interstate highways had to go over mountains they would become little more than winding paths. And when they crossed a river there would be no bridge but only a place where the river was shallow; the road would end on one riverbank and start again on the other side, so that travelers had to wade through the water.

Nobody in his right mind would travel a long distance alone. People would form caravans and bring armed guards along for safety. Not only could the weather be bad (too wet or terribly hot), there were also wild animals such as lions and bears, and there were always outlaws and bandits waiting to attack travelers. People often traveled at night because it was cooler and they couldn't be spotted as easily by robbers.

And travel was slow. Abraham and his family had to travel about 1,100 miles from Ur to Shechem. They had to follow the river because they needed water; if they could have gone straight it would have been only about 600 miles.

But in Old Testament times people could travel only about nine or ten miles per day (on very good days on level terrain perhaps twenty miles). The fastest Abraham could have made the trip was in about four months! We could fly 1,100 miles in a few hours or drive it in a couple of days.

This here's the trail from Ur to Shechem – the same one Abraham took. Whaddaya think of the camel? My finest model yet. Smooth ride. Desert-dynamic styling. Where was I? Oh, yes. Abraham. To get to the Promised Land, he traveled over a thousand miles – 1,100 to be exact – going only nine miles a day. Took him four months. Yup. If he'd had one of our fine camel models here, it would've taken him only three, three-and-half months tops. By the way, did you ever hear the one about…BLAH BLAH BLAH.

I don't think this camel ride is going to be such a hot idea…

I wonder if this program has a mute button.

Today, a mosque stands on top of the cave where Abraham and Sarah were buried.

Abraham's Family
Genesis

When they finally came to Canaan, Abraham was already old enough to be a great-grand-father – but he and Sarah had never had any children. (Read Genesis 12:4 to find out how old Abraham was.) And these people who were used to living in fancy houses in the city now had to live in tents.

The most important thing that ever happened to Abraham was that God made an agreement (called a "covenant") with him. God promised Abraham that he would have as many descendants (children, grandchildren, great-grandchildren, and so on) as there are stars – which nobody can count! That sounded strange, because Abraham didn't even have one child!

God also promised that one day Abraham's descendants would own all of Canaan – even though Abraham didn't own one square inch of the land yet. And God promised Abraham that he would one day become a blessing to the whole world.

God has kept his promises! First of all, Abraham did get a son, Isaac. If you think your parents are old, think of Isaac: When Isaac was born his father was one hundred years old, and his mother ninety! Abraham's descendants are the Jews, some of whom today once again live in Canaan (now called Israel). And through the most important one of his descendants, Jesus, Abraham has become a blessing to the whole world! *Genesis 15:1-6*
Genesis 21:1-7

Adventure Readings:
- Abraham and Lot: **Genesis 13-14**
- Hagar and Ishmael: **Genesis 16**
- The destruction of Sodom and Gomorrah: **Genesis 18:1-33, 19:1, 12-29**
- Hagar and Ishmael are sent away: **Genesis 21:8-20**
- God asks Abraham to sacrifice Isaac: **Genesis 22:1-19**

Arabian nomads still live in tents like these. They're as long as my neighbor's motorhome — but without turn signals.

In 1922, archaeologist Leonard Woolley excavated Ur and found the 4,500-year-old remains of servants who were killed so they could keep their royal masters company in the tomb.

Jacob had to work seven years before he could marry his first wife, Leah, and seven years after he married his second wife, Rachel. (Genesis 29:14-30)

ABRAHAM'S PLACE

Isaac had two sons of his own: Esau and Jacob. Esau was a tough, hairy man who loved to hunt. Jacob was more the quiet type and could be sneaky.

In Old Testament times, the oldest son inherited everything his father owned and became responsible for the rest of the family. So Esau, because he was the oldest, would inherit his father's possessions and receive a special blessing.

Jacob was jealous, so one day when Esau came home very hungry, he talked Esau into trading his "birthright" (the rights that came with being the oldest) for, of all things, a bowl of stew! *Genesis 25:19-34*

In spite of the sneaky way in which Jacob had talked Esau out of his birthright, God treated Jacob as the oldest and, in a dream, made the same promises to him that God had made to Abraham: He would become a large nation who would one day own all of Canaan, and one day he would become a blessing to the whole world.
Genesis 27:1-40 *Genesis 27:41-31:21*

Jacob's Name Change

Jacob's name comes from a word that means "to cheat" – not very flattering! But God gave Jacob a wonderful new name: Israel, which means "Prince of God." In the Old Testament, Abraham's descendants are usually called "Israelites" and the whole nation is called "Israel."

BLAH BLAH BLAH BLAH BLAH…

Is Max short for maxed-out mouth?

I'd rather listen to Professor Ed any day!

Bye, Max! We gotta blitz!

27

Joseph
Genesis

Jacob had twelve sons and one daughter – poor girl! Jacob's youngest sons were Joseph and Benjamin, and because they were the sons of his favorite wife (Jacob had several wives) Jacob spoiled them – especially Joseph.

He gave Joseph a colorful coat, very different from the work clothes of his brothers. In fact, Joseph didn't do a lot of work. He became proud and difficult to live with, and he wasn't very popular with his brothers.

But to top it all off, Joseph had two dreams in which his brothers and even his father were bowing down to him. And Joseph made the mistake of telling everybody about his dreams.

That was too much for his brothers. One day Joseph went to visit them in the field (not to help them with their work but just to see how they were doing), and when his brothers saw Joseph coming they decided then and there to kill him.

They threw him in a cistern, a deep pit for storing water (which fortunately was dry), and they intended to leave him there to die. But then his brothers decided that they might as well make some money while they were getting rid of Joseph, so they pulled Joseph back out of the pit and sold him to some traders who were on their way down to Egypt.

They should have left him in the pit, because now Joseph's dreams could (and would) come true!
Genesis 37:1-36

Cistern

Brethren

•Dothan

Ninety-nine percent of Egypt's people live along the Nile on less than four percent of her land.

Shechem •

Altar

Bethel •

Ephrath
(Bethlehem)

Hebron •

Dead
Sea

Later in Egypt

Sold as a slave...

In prison...

Vice-Pharoah

Near the ancient city of Gezer, between Jerusalem and the Mediterranean Sea, skeletons have been found in a large cistern, which shows that these cisterns were used to get rid of people in Old Testament times!

In Egypt
Genesis/Exodus

In Egypt, Joseph was sold as a slave. God had a plan for Joseph, and surprisingly, the spoiled brat from Canaan proved that he could work. His master was so impressed that he made Joseph manager of his property.

His master's wife fell in love with Joseph. But Joseph didn't want to do anything God would not approve of, so he didn't return her affection. This made her so mad that she lied about Joseph and had him thrown in prison.

But then Pharaoh, the king of Egypt, got angry at two important officials, and he put them in the same prison as Joseph.

These two men each had a strange dream, and Joseph explained to them what the dreams meant: The royal baker would be hanged, but the cupbearer would get his job back. Joseph turned out to be right, but when the cupbearer went back to his job, he promptly forgot about Joseph. (A cupbearer served the king his wine – a very important job because he had to keep the Pharaoh from being poisoned.)

Hieroglyphics are a kind of picture writing the Egyptians used. Joseph probably had to learn this.

Inside one of the great temples of ancient Egypt. A person standing in this picture next to the pillar in front would only be 1/4 inch (6 mm) tall!

Egypt

Egypt is a large country, about the size of Texas, Oklahoma, and Arkansas together. But people can live in only a very small part of the country, right along the Nile River, in an area about one-third the size of Oklahoma. The rest is desert, where people cannot live.

Until the Aswan Dam was built in the twentieth century, the Nile would rise each year as much as twenty-three feet (about the height of a two-story house!), and the land on both sides of the river would be flooded for three or four months. This was good, because it made the land fertile.

In Old Testament times, Egypt was a powerful country, ruled by the Pharaoh, who was looked up to as a god. The Egyptians also believed that the earth and the sky and the Nile were gods, and they built great temples along the Nile for their gods.

Dreams were very important to Egyptians. They even had books to help people interpret them.

MEDITERRANEAN SEA

EGYPT

RED SEA

But two years later, Pharaoh had a strange dream (there are lots of dreams in the story about Joseph!). He dreamed about seven beautiful, fat cows and seven skinny, ugly cows that ate the fat cows.

When no one could explain the dream, the cupbearer suddenly remembered how Joseph had told him what his dream had meant. Joseph was called out of prison and explained Pharaoh's dream: There would be seven "fat" years, followed by seven years of famine.

Joseph told Pharaoh that during the seven fat years he should put a part of each year's harvest in great bins, so that there would be grain during the seven years of famine. The Pharaoh liked the idea so much that he put Joseph in charge of Egypt as vice-pharaoh, and because of Joseph's plan there was enough food in Egypt during the seven years of famine.

Genesis 41:1-57

Medieval pilgrims called the pyramids "Joseph-barns" because they believed Joseph stored grain in them.

But Joseph didn't only save Egypt – he also saved his own brothers and his father! The famine that came to Egypt also struck Canaan. When Joseph's father, Jacob, heard that there was grain in Egypt, he sent Joseph's brothers to Egypt to buy some.

And there they met Joseph again – but they didn't realize that the important Egyptian they talked with was Joseph. Did Joseph take revenge? No, he taught his brothers a lesson they never forgot! It's a long story that should be read as a whole. 🐸 *Genesis 42:1-46:4*

Joseph invited his whole family to move down to Egypt. The Pharaoh even sent carts for them to travel in! And that's how at the end of the book of Genesis all of Abraham's descendants were living in Egypt rather than in the Promised Land, Canaan.

When Jacob died, Joseph and his brothers took him back to Canaan and buried him there. But Joseph, like all important Egyptians, was embalmed and buried as a mummy when he died. 🐸 *Genesis 49:29-50:3*
🐸*Genesis 50:15-26*

WHOA! This is better than the view from the Sears Tower!

I think I found an entrance!

The first structure built in Egypt larger than the pyramids is the Aswan Dam, finished in 1971. It contains enough material for seventeen great pyramids.

Careful you guys!

The Valley of the Kings, where many Pharaohs were buried. It was once spectacularly beautiful, but time and grave robbers have made it what it is today. (See page 34.)

The Pyramids

The pyramids in Egypt were built as tombs for the Pharaohs. When Joseph arrived in Egypt the pyramids had already been standing for hundreds of years, so Joseph and the Israelites saw the same pyramids we see today (except that the pyramids were still covered with smooth limestone, which since has been removed for use in other building projects).

The largest pyramid, the Great Pyramid at Giza, was 481 feet tall before its top was removed, and each side was 756 feet long. The Great Pyramid covers more ground than the Louisiana Superdome!

The Great Pyramid is solid rock, except for a few passageways inside. It is made up of almost 2,500,000 gigantic blocks of stone, each one weighing between 5,000 and 30,000 pounds.

Perhaps the pyramids were built by farmers who couldn't work during the months that the Nile flooded their fields. Nobody knows for sure how the enormous blocks of stone were put into place – without machines or cranes. Perhaps the stones were put on rollers and pushed and pulled up on ramps made of sand, which were later removed.

If you wanted to build the Great Pyramid today, it would take about six years and cost several billion dollars.

Come on, Brad! Can't you make it up?

Couldn't we just blitz to the top?

Because many people have been hurt or killed trying to climb the pyramids, it is now illegal to climb them.

33

Mummies

The Egyptians believed that people lived after death. They preserved people by mummifying their bodies (after they died).

They would remove the internal organs such as the stomach, which were carefully put in jars, and later also the brain, which was pulled out through a hole made in the skull. The body was then filled with resin (similar to the sticky sap that comes out of a pine tree) and linen.

If the mummy had been an important person, such as a pharaoh or a high official, it would be put in a large box (sometimes several boxes, one inside the other) called a sarcophagus.

The mummies were buried with food and lots of valuable things made of gold and precious stones so that they would have food and money on the trip through the hereafter.

Of course, everybody knew that Pharaohs and other important people were buried with valuable things, so a lot of people tried to find the graves and rob them. One grave that was never robbed was that of King Tutankhamen (better known as King Tut). In 1922 his grave was found with marvelous treasures inside. And King Tut had not even been a very important pharaoh!

Later (long after the time of Joseph) the Egyptians also began to embalm animals they believed to represent gods, such as cats and dogs, crocodiles, birds, and even bulls! Think how big the sarcophagus for a bull had to be!

Much, much later, the Arabs would dig up mummies, break them into pieces, and use them as firewood. The mummies burned well because of the resin inside them.

Stranger yet, until about three hundred years ago, ancient mummies from Egypt were sent to Europe where they were ground into a powder that was used as medicine.

This is the mummy of Pharaoh Ramses II. We don't know where his daddy is.

When Jacob and his family moved to Egypt, there were seventy people. When the Israelites left Egypt 400 years later, there were over two million!

Hello?

Calm down, Chip. It's only Brad. Didn't you see his tennis shoes?

AEEIOU!

C-o-m-e h-e-r-e, little boy! I'm your mummy!

Archaeology

In any place where people live, they leave things behind. Most of those things will simply rot away (especially in places that have a lot of rain), but other things can last for thousands of years – for example, pieces of dishes and cups and jewelry and things made of metal.

Archaeology is the study of things left behind by people from the past. Most of archaeology is simply hard work. Archaeologists will spend months and years slowly and carefully digging to find a few pieces of pottery. From the small things they find they can get a good idea of how people lived in the past.

But once in a while archaeology can be quite exciting. The people who discovered King Tut's tomb in Egypt couldn't believe what they saw when they broke through the wall and found the marvelous things inside.

In Bible lands, you'll often see small hills (called "tells") where there used to be a city in ancient times. Thousands of years ago, a small city was built there, which was destroyed by fire or by enemies. A new city was built on top of the ruins of the old city. The new city was destroyed again, and yet another city built on top of it.

After a while, the rubble from all those cities formed a hill, and often people would forget that once that hill was a city. But in that hill are pieces of pottery and sometimes weapons that help archaeologists understand how the people of that city once lived.

Egyptian women used many of the cosmetics we use today, including eye shadow, lipstick, rouge, and even red fingernail polish made from the crushed leaves of henna.

Valley of the Kings again (what about the queens?). These temples were already hundreds of years old when the Israelites left Egypt.

Moses

Exodus

The book of Genesis ended with the arrival in Egypt of Jacob's family (also called the Israelites). The book of Exodus jumps to a time 400 years later, when the Israelites (who were called "Hebrews" by the Egyptians) had grown from just a few people into a large nation.

The Pharaoh who now ruled Egypt didn't remember Joseph and how Joseph had saved Egypt 400 years ago. He was just worried because there were too many Israelites. Pharaoh was afraid that if there ever was a war the Israelites would help his enemies.

He decided to make life as difficult as he could for the Israelites. He hoped that that would make them weak. He made the Israelites slaves and forced them to build whole cities – with bricks they had to make themselves.

But the more Pharaoh mistreated them, the larger and stronger the Israelite nation became. Finally the Pharaoh gave an order that any Israelite boys who were born should be thrown in the Nile. ☙ *Exodus 1:1-22*

This brick may have been made by the Israelites out of straw and clay from the Nile River. It's stamped with the Good Housekeeping Seal of Approval (actually, the royal seal of Ramses II).

Exodus means "leaving, going out" and the book of Exodus tells us how the Israelites left Egypt to go back to Canaan.

But God hadn't forgotten the Israelites and his promises to Abraham. One day an Israelite boy was born who wasn't killed. His parents knew that it was wrong to kill the baby, so they obeyed God rather than Pharaoh. They did throw him in the Nile, as Pharaoh had told them to do – but safely inside a basket made from papyrus reeds covered with tar! His sister, Miriam, kept an eye on the basket.

Then God arranged for Pharaoh's daughter to come down to the Nile to take a bath just as the little baby was floating down the river in his basket. Pharaoh's daughter adopted the boy and called him Moses. He grew up near the court of the Pharaoh, where he got a very good education. 🐸 *Exodus 2:1-10*

One day, when Moses was already forty years old, he saw an Egyptian beating a Hebrew. He got so mad that he killed the Egyptian. The Pharaoh didn't like it, of course, and Moses had to run away to save his life.

He went to Midian, east of Egypt, where for forty years he was a shepherd. But it wasn't wasted time. The country Moses got to know so well during those forty years was the same country through which he would later lead the Israelites on their way back to Canaan! 🐸 *Exodus 2:11-25*

This is a statue of Pharaoh Ramses II before he became a mummy (see page 34). We still don't know where his daddy is.

Blub, Why? Why me?

It's only a hologram. It's only a hologram.

Outta my face, frog breath.

Shh! Someone's coming!

Grrr. This dumb control box needs more RAM!

The Plagues

Exodus

Gurgle. Burp.

I didn't know the Nile had Jacuzzi action.

How'd this frog get in here?

When do I meet Kermit?

W hen Moses was about eighty years old, he was finally ready for the job God had planned for him. God spoke to him from a bush that was on fire – but didn't burn up! God told Moses to go back to Egypt and to tell the Pharaoh that God said, "Let my people go!"

Moses had all kinds of excuses why God should not send him back to Egypt. The biggest excuse was that he was not a very good speaker. So God sent Aaron, Moses' older brother, to meet him, and together Moses and Aaron went to the Pharaoh. *Exodus 3:1-4:20 Exodus 4:27-31*

But Pharaoh was stubborn and said, "No! I won't let the Israelites go." In fact, he made life even more miserable for the Israelites! *Exodus 5:1-6:12*

So God sent ten plagues – ten terrible things that happened to the Egyptians, but not to the Israelites.

The water in the Nile turned into blood, the land was covered with frogs, then came mosquitoes and flies. The animals became sick and died, and everybody got sores all over their bodies. It hailed, and grasshoppers ate up all the trees and plants. Then it became totally dark.

Imagine what it must have been like for the Egyptians to see the river that made their crops grow turn into blood. Or waking up with fifty frogs in their bed and one or two sitting on their face. Or having a gezillion mosquitoes or flies in their house so they couldn't even sit down without squashing them or take a bite without chomping on a fly. *Exodus 7:14-11:10*

In ancient Hebrew fairy tales, the frog is a very wise animal with magical powers.

To understand how important all this was, remember that the Egyptians thought that the Pharaoh was a god, who was supposed to keep the world running smoothly.

God sent the ten plagues to show that he was more powerful than Pharaoh. Pharaoh couldn't protect the Nile, the source of life for Egypt. He couldn't even protect his people from frogs, mosquitoes, and flies. Pharaoh could only watch helplessly as the farm animals got sick and the crops were destroyed by hail and locusts.

And finally, God was more powerful than both the Pharaoh and the sun god when total darkness came over the land.

But Pharaoh was stubborn. He still refused to let God's people go – until the tenth and last plague, when Pharaoh's oldest son died, as well as the oldest son in every Egyptian family. But God had told the Israelites to put some blood from a lamb on their doorposts, and not one of the Israelites' oldest sons died! From then on, the Israelites celebrated this event every year; it was called the Passover because God's angel passed over the homes of the Israelites and spared their first-born sons.

Exodus 11:1-8   *Exodus 12:1-13; 29-30*

The Egyptians had many gods – the Nile River god, the frog god, the cow and bull gods, the sun god, and the Pharaoh god. Through the plagues, the Lord God of Israel proved he was stronger than all these gods!

The Exodus

Exodus

The Egyptians had had enough. They were glad to see the Israelites go – so glad that they gave the Israelites silver and gold and clothing (remember, the Israelites had been slaves who had nothing!).

Imagine several million people getting ready to move, with large herds of farm animals and everything else they now owned. It was noisy and smelly and confusing. But God was in charge. *Exodus 12:31-42*

Which way did the Israelites travel to Canaan? There was a direct road from Egypt to Canaan along the coast of the Mediterranean Sea. But that road ran through the country of the Philistines, and the Israelites weren't ready to fight the Philistines yet.

Instead, they went east and south into the Sinai Peninsula. But there was a problem: the Red Sea blocked their way. And to make things worse, Pharaoh now was sorry that he had let the Israelites go, and he chased them with his army – with horses and chariots and troops – to bring them back to Egypt.

Q: Why was the Red Sea angry?

A: The children of Israel crossed it.

Look, Mom, a school of people!

Wow! Crossing the Red Sea with the Israelites is better than going to Sea World!

Groan. Never thought I could be camel sick and seasick at the same time.

The two-wheeled Egyptian war chariot was light, fast, and very dangerous to drive — sort of like my brother's motorcycle.

Because it lies between hot deserts, the water temperature of the Red Sea reaches 85° F. (29° C.) in the summer.

The Israelites were caught between the Red Sea and Pharaoh's army. They were scared and began to complain that maybe this wasn't such a good idea after all. Maybe they should have stayed in Egypt. But Moses stretched his staff over the sea and a strong wind pushed the water back so that the Israelites had a dry path through the sea. Then, when the Egyptians tried to follow them, the sea once again covered the dry path, and the Egyptian army drowned.

The Israelites were free at last!

Exodus 13:17–14:31

There's something humany going on here.

Look! The Egyptians are coming! Pretty soon they'll be fish bait!

Isn't he c-u-t-e? Where'd you get him, Chip?

I think he's a holographic computer glitch. I'm calling him Froggo!

At Sinai

The Israelites were free, but it didn't take long before they started to grumble. They complained that there wasn't enough water, so God gave them water. They complained because there wasn't enough food – so God gave them food. Each morning the ground around the camp was white with flakes that looked like frost (not quite the same thing as frosted flakes, although they were sweet). It was called manna, and God sent it every day (except on the Sabbath) for as long as the Israelites were in the wilderness.

But after a while the Israelites even complained about the manna – they remembered the onions and cucumbers they ate in Egypt. Some of the people even wanted to go back just because they didn't like the food God gave them! But God loved the Israelites even when they complained a lot.

Exodus 16:1-35

After they had been traveling through the wilderness for three months, they came to a mountain called Sinai (the same mountain where Moses had talked with God in the burning bush). There at Mount Sinai God made an agreement (called a "covenant") with the Israelites.

Rumble grumble.

Is your stomach grumbling? You don't look too well.

God told Moses to have the Israelites stand around the mountain and God would speak to them. Then, as they stood waiting, a dark cloud covered the mountain and they heard what sounded like a very loud trumpet blast. The Israelites were so frightened by the noise that they said to Moses: "You tell us what God says. Don't let him speak to us, because we're afraid we'll die if he does." *Exodus 19:1-25*

So God talked to Moses and gave Moses laws for the people of Israel. Of all the laws God gave Moses we are most familiar with the Ten Commandments. God himself wrote the Ten Commandments on two large, flat stones called "tablets." The Ten Commandments were to Israel kind of like what the Constitution is to Americans. *Exodus 20:1-21*

Mount Sinai

Listen! Froggo does animal impersonations!

Woof! Woof!

Are you gwumbling?

Me not gwumbling. Are you gwumbling?

Me not gwumbling. Maybe the camel is gwumbling. Are you gwumbling?

The Ten Commandments for Young People

1. You may not love anyone or anything more than you love God.

2. You may not worship, or put more importance on, any person or thing, other than God. You must worship only the Lord, not your parents, not a friend, not a movie star or sports hero, not a cat or boat or skateboard. Nothing.

3. You may not swear. Use God's holy name only in a loving way, never to express anger or frustration.

4. One day of your week should be set aside for rest and the worship of God. Work six days of the week only. You need a special day set aside to relax and meet with other Christians.

5. Be respectful to your parents. Love them, and the Lord will reward you with long life.

6. You may not hate other people; don't ever think of hurting someone else in any way.

7. Keep your thoughts and actions pure. Sex is a gift of God to married couples.

8. You may not take and keep anything that doesn't belong to you.

9. You may not tell lies, especially when that lie will hurt someone else.

10. You may not be jealous of what others have. You may not be jealous of your friend's new game or clothes or the big house your neighbor lives in. Be satisfied with what you have.

God talked to Moses on the mountain for forty days – almost six weeks! The people down below began to wonder what had happened to Moses. They told Aaron, Moses' brother, "Look, we don't know what happened to Moses, but we don't think he is coming back. And we don't see God, so he probably isn't around either. Why don't we give you all the gold we have and you melt it down and make a statue of a calf, and we'll call that our god!"

Aaron listened to the people and made the statue. And while God was still talking to Moses on the mountaintop, the people began dancing around the statue and worshiping it.

While they were dancing and making noise, Moses came down from the mountain. When he saw what they were doing, he got so angry that he smashed the stones on which God had written the Ten Commandments. Then he took the statue of the calf, broke it into pieces, and ground it up into dust.

Exodus 32:1-35

At about the same time as Moses, an ancient king named Hammurabi also established laws for his people to follow, but his laws did not come directly from God.

NO MORE MANNA
NO MORE MOSES

LONG LIVE THE
GOLD CALF!

The Tabernacle

Exodus

But God is patient – much more patient than you or I! He still wanted to be Israel's God, and he still wanted the Israelites to be his people. He wrote the Ten Commandments again on two new flat pieces of stone. *Exodus 34:1-35*

He also told Moses to build a place where the Israelites could worship God. It wasn't going to be a temple, because it would have been impossible to carry a large stone building around as the Israelites traveled through the wilderness. God told Moses to build a portable place of worship called the "tabernacle." The tabernacle was easy to take apart when the Israelites moved on and it was easy to put back together when the Israelites stopped.

The Israelites had given Aaron gold to make the golden calf, but now they gave gold and silver and many other things for the building of the tabernacle. Moses put the two new tablets of the Law inside a large, beautiful box, called the "ark of the covenant," which was placed in the tabernacle.
Exodus 35:4-19; 40:1-38

No one knows what finally happened to the Ark of the Covenant. It disappeared without a trace.

Tabernacle

The Israelites had only one place where they came to worship God – the tabernacle. Only the priests were allowed to go inside, and the people stayed outside. The tabernacle was also called "the Tent of Meeting," because God met with his people there.

The tabernacle stood inside a courtyard that was about one-fourth the size of a football field. In the courtyard the priests burned the animals that were sacrificed to God on the altar. (This happened every day, several times a day – the camp must have smelled terrible!)

The tabernacle itself was a tent with two rooms. The larger one in front was called the Holy Place, and the priests went in and out of it every day.

The smaller room in the back was called the Most Holy Place. In the Most Holy Place stood the ark of the covenant. Only the High Priest could go into the Most Holy Place, and only once a year, on the Day of Atonement.

The tabernacle was used for several hundred years, until King Solomon built the temple in Jerusalem.

On the Day of Atonement, one goat was sacrificed as a sin offering and another goat was driven into the desert to show that the peoples' sins had been sent away. That's where we get our word scapegoat.

Get him! Get him! He's over here!

Twenty bucks, it's yours! OK, OK, for you – ten bucks!

The Law
Leviticus/Numbers

According to Jewish tradition, God gave Moses 613 laws, which are written down in the first five books of the Bible.

Leviticus

The book of Leviticus doesn't tell a story. It talks about the laws God gave to Moses for the people of Israel. "Leviticus" means "about the Levites." God made one group of Israelites, the tribe of Levi, responsible for everything that had to do with the worship of God and the laws of God.

The Law was very important for the Israelites. In Egypt, they had lived by Egyptian rules and laws. Now they were on their own and they needed new rules to live by.

God told the Israelites how they should live with each other, how they should treat each other, and how they should worship God.

The Law also told the Israelites how to bring sacrifices to God, how to deal with thieves, what they shouldn't eat if they wanted to stay healthy, and many other things.

God's laws were not rules God made up because he wanted to make life difficult for the Israelites. Exactly the opposite! God gave laws to help the Israelites to live together peacefully.

Because the Israelites were God's people, they should live differently than other people who did not know God. They were to be a holy people.

The Israelites weren't very good at keeping the law. God often had to punish them so that they would turn back to God and to his law.

Adventure Reading:
- What you do makes a difference!: **Leviticus 26:3-22**

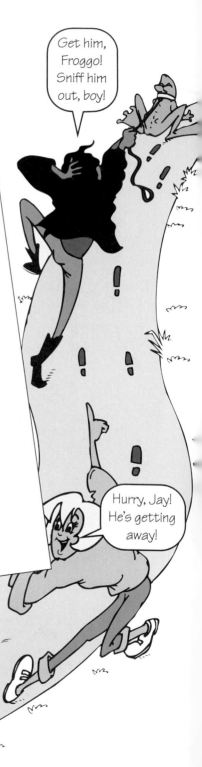

Get him, Froggo! Sniff him out, boy!

Hurry, Jay! He's getting away!

Let's send the Law after him.

Numbers

The book of Numbers begins with a census, taken when the people were still at Sinai. (When all the people of a country or nation are counted, it is called a census. In the United States a census is taken every ten years.) That is why this book is called "Numbers."

The people were counted because the Israelites would soon have to fight the people of Canaan. They had to put together an army, and Moses had to know how many men there were who could be soldiers.

Also, when they reached Canaan, each of the twelve tribes would be given part of the land, and Moses had to know how much land each tribe needed.

Very good tackle, my son. What tribe are you from? You will make a very fine addition to our army.

OK, OK! For you — two bucks!

Come to papa!

The Twelve Tribes of Israel

Remember that Jacob had twelve sons. Each of these twelve sons had a family, and while the Israelites were in Egypt, these twelve families became very large and were called "tribes."

Here is the list of tribes as they were counted in the census:

Reuben
Simeon
Judah
Issachar

Zebulun
Benjamin
Dan
Asher

Gad
Naphtali
Ephraim
Manasseh

Why is there no tribe of Joseph? The last two tribes, Ephraim and Manasseh, are named after Joseph's two sons, so that there are actually two tribes of Joseph. There is also no tribe of Levi, because the Levites weren't supposed to be soldiers, and when the Israelites came to Canaan, the Levites would not own land; they would live among the other tribes to help them worship God.

Many ancient kings took a census of their people to see how much money they could collect in taxes.

The 12 Spies

At last, the Israelites were ready to move on from Sinai and start the trip to Canaan, the Promised Land. All went well, except that the Israelites grumbled a lot about their food. They were tired of the manna and remembered how good the fish and the melons and onions and garlic in Egypt had been – they actually thought about going back!

🐸 *Numbers 11:1-25, 31-35*

🐸 **Adventure Reading:**

• The Great Blessing: **Numbers 6:22-27**

Finally the Israelites reached the southern border of Canaan. But before going in to conquer the land, the Israelites sent twelve spies to take a look.

When the spies came back forty days later they told Moses and the Israelites, "The land flows with milk and honey"! To us that sounds messy and sticky, but it meant that the land was very good to live in and to grow things in.

But, the spies said, the people are something else! They are giants who live in big, strong cities. If we attack them, they will kill us.

The oldest use of an alphabet that archaeologists have found came from the Sinai desert. The writing was done at least two hundred years before the Israelites wandered there.

Geffyer foofout tamym ouf!

There are no spies hiding behind this picture

Whaddaya staring at, kid? Haven't ya seen a palm tree before?

The spies may have seen jewelry like this on the Canaanite women. Back then, women pierced their ears and sometimes their noses, too!

nly two of the twelve spies, Joshua and Caleb, told the Israelites that with God's help the Israelites could attack and win.

But the people listened to the other spies and ignored Caleb and Joshua. They started wailing and refused to go on. They even wanted to choose a different leader and go back to Egypt!

God became angry with the Israelites because they simply did not believe that God could and would keep his promise and give the land of Canaan to them. He told them that all Israelites who were twenty years old or older would die in the wilderness – except Caleb and Joshua, who had believed God.

The Israelites would have to wander around from place to place in the wilderness before God would help them conquer the people of Canaan.

When the people heard this, they realized that they had made a big mistake. They decided to try to attack the Canaanites and Amalekites anyway – but without God's help they didn't have a chance!

Numbers 13:1-14:45

Adventure Reading:
• The Bronze Snake: **Numbers 21:1-9**

These are Canaanite lawn ornaments – NOT. We wanted to put in some pictures of interesting things like clothing. The problem is, stuff made of leather and cloth and wood rots away over the centuries, so that what's left is mostly things made of stone.

Anyway, on the left is a stone from a Canaanite temple with hands reaching to the moon. Next to it is a stone sarcophagus (coffin) shaped like a human being. On the right are two incense burners. People used incense in worship and for perfume to cover up their B.O. (Talk about stink! Most people back then hardly ever took baths.)

40 Years in the Wilderness

Numbers

The Israelites camped in the wilderness for forty years. During those forty years, the Israelites met some of their new neighbors, but the neighborhood didn't turn out to be very friendly. They had trouble with the Edomites, the Amorites, and several other small nations around Canaan.

The Israelites turned out to be good fighters, and with the Lord's help they defeated several of the small nations that tried to keep Israel away from Canaan. In fact, the king of Moab became so afraid that he sent for Balaam, a man who was believed to have a special relationship with the gods.

The king of Moab asked Balaam to put a curse on Israel. So Balaam went on his donkey to see the king of Moab, a trip that probably took about three weeks. On the way God spoke to Balaam, and Balaam's donkey turned out to be smarter than Balaam: it saw the angel of the Lord long before Balaam did and talked to Balaam!

When Balaam finally tried to curse the Israelites, God wouldn't let him – Balaam could only bless the Israelites!

Numbers 22:1-6, 20-41
Numbers 23:7-12

The Edomites were descendants of Esau; the Moabites and Ammonites were descendants of Lot (Abraham's nephew).

Israel's Neighbors

Israel's neighbors are often mentioned in the Bible. It wasn't a fun neighborhood – nobody really got along with anybody else, especially not with the Israelites!

Syrians
(in Syria)

Arameans
(in Aram, another name for Syria)

Phoenicians
(in Phoenicia)

Lost*

Ammonites
(in Ammon)

Amorites
(east of Canaan)

Mediterranean Sea

Dead Sea

Moabites
(in Moab)

Philistines
(in Philistia)

Edomites
(in Edom)

Mosquito–bites
(on my arm)

Termites, pillow fights, satellites.

From Down South

Midianites
(in Midian)

The word "Palestine" comes from "Philistine"; it originally meant "the place where the Philistines live."

*We don't know exactly where they lived.

Getting Ready to Conquer

Deuteronomy

Most people in the time of Moses did not live much longer than fifty years.

Israel now was ready to enter the Promised Land and conquer it. But Moses (who was by now 120 years old!) wanted to make sure that the Israelites remembered all the things God had told their parents at Sinai forty years earlier.

Moses talked to the Israelites about the law for a whole week! His sermon takes up almost all of the book of Deuteronomy (Deuteronomy means "second law").

Moses gave them the Ten Commandments again (Deuteronomy 5) and told them what was the most important thing of all:

Hear, O Israel: The Lord our God, the Lord is one. Love the Lord your God with all your heart and with all your soul and with all your strength. (Deuteronomy 6:4-5)

Moses also reminded the Israelites that God wanted them to get rid of all the people who were living in Canaan, and that after Moses died, Joshua would take over as the leader of Israel.

Moses' job was finished. He died just before the Israelites under Joshua entered Canaan.

Deuteronomy 7:1-16   Numbers 27:12-23
Deuteronomy 34:1-12

I'll never complain about two-hour church services again.

I can't believe I listened to the whole thing...

The Canaanites

The Canaanites had many gods, but the most important ones were Baal, Astarte, and Dagon. The worship of these gods often involved things the Israelites knew were evil – even human sacrifices.

The Canaanites weren't one big nation. They lived in cities, each with its own king. To us, the Canaanite cities wouldn't seem large. Many were not larger than the size of about twenty football fields (twenty-five acres). But the city walls were enormous – up to almost ten yards thick.

Hazor, the largest city in Canaan, was still less than one-fourth square mile in size (or about eight or ten of our city blocks). It was surrounded by walls made of earth that were 100 feet thick at the bottom! Those walls were necessary to keep attacking armies from capturing the city.

One of the most important things for a city was to have a well or a spring inside the walls, so that when the city was surrounded by enemies the people would still have water.

Q: Who, besides Adam and
Eve, had no parents?

A: Joshua, the son of Nun.

This Canaanite altar is about twenty-seven feet across and was used for animal and human sacrifices.

What's up, Rebecca?

Look! God's making a path through the Jordan River!

PATH THROUGH THE JORDAN RIVER

River? Did I hear somebody say river?

Joshua Captures Jericho

Joshua

River Out. Watch Your Step.

Hang on, Chip. Let me read this sign.

Whee!

I'm coming! I'm coming!

Wait for me!

Tracy, I can't see where I'm going!

Brad, watch your head!

Jericho is probably the oldest city in the world.

Joshua Was Here

Joshua and the Israelites were camped at the Jordan River, across from Jericho. Joshua sent spies into the land, as Moses had done forty years earlier.

But this time the spies had a very different report; they said, "Let's do it – with God's help!"

Adventure Reading:

• Rahab and the Spies: **Joshua 2:1-24**

The first thing they had to do was cross the Jordan River. The priests who carried the ark of the covenant simply walked into the river, and as soon as their feet touched the water, the river stopped running so that the Israelites could walk across the dry riverbed.

Joshua 3:1-17

Now they stood before the first Canaanite city: Jericho. The people of Jericho weren't too terribly worried. Their walls were strong, and the soldiers of Jericho would be able to keep the Israelites from climbing over the wall.

But what happened was not at all what they expected. The Israelite army didn't try to climb the walls – they simply walked silently around the city, once a day for six days.

Then, on the seventh day, just when the people in Jericho were getting used to seeing the Israelites going around and around, the Israelites did something different. This time seven priests carrying trumpets walked with the soldiers, and the ark of the covenant was also carried along.

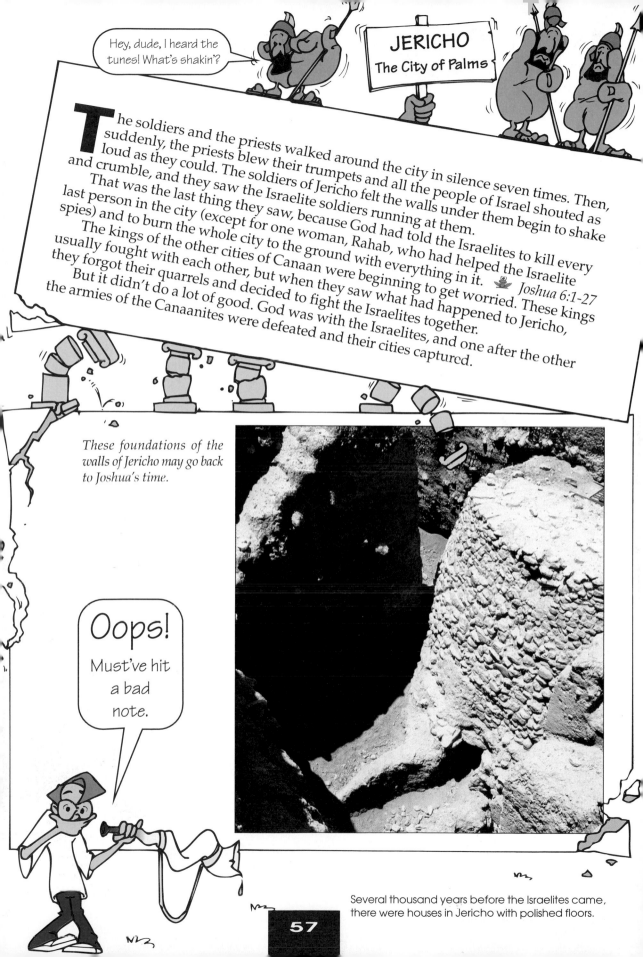

Hey, dude, I heard the tunes! What's shakin'?

JERICHO
The City of Palms

The soldiers and the priests walked around the city in silence seven times. Then, suddenly, the priests blew their trumpets and all the people of Israel shouted as loud as they could. The soldiers of Jericho felt the walls under them begin to shake and crumble, and they saw the Israelite soldiers running at them.

That was the last thing they saw, because God had told the Israelites to kill every last person in the city (except for one woman, Rahab, who had helped the Israelite spies) and to burn the whole city to the ground with everything in it.
Joshua 6:1-27

The kings of the other cities of Canaan were beginning to get worried. These kings usually fought with each other, but when they saw what had happened to Jericho, they forgot their quarrels and decided to fight the Israelites together.

But it didn't do a lot of good. God was with the Israelites, and one after the other the armies of the Canaanites were defeated and their cities captured.

These foundations of the walls of Jericho may go back to Joshua's time.

Oops! Must've hit a bad note.

Several thousand years before the Israelites came, there were houses in Jericho with polished floors.

The Promised Land

Joshua

If a family had only daughters and no sons, their land would be passed on to the daughters, but only if they married someone from the same tribe.

The land of Canaan was divided among the tribes by lot, which is like picking names out of a hat.

After Jericho, Joshua and the Israelites went west and captured Ai. They kept going west to Gibeon, where they battled with the armies of several kings. During this battle Joshua asked God to make the sun stand still so that the Israelites would have enough time to defeat the enemies. The sun stood still for about a whole day, and the Israelites defeated their enemies.

🐸 *Joshua 10:1-15*

Now Joshua and the Israelites were in control of the middle part of the country. That meant that the kings from the north of Canaan couldn't help the kings of the south when the Israelites attacked them. Joshua and the Israelites first defeated the kings in the south, then the kings in the north.

🐸 **Adventure Reading:**
  • The sad story of Achan: **Joshua 7-8**

Joshua never completely conquered Canaan. Several cities (including Jerusalem) wouldn't be captured until almost 400 years later. But at the end of Joshua's life the Israelites owned enough of the land to be able to divide it among the twelve tribes.

Before Joshua died, the people renewed the covenant that God had made with their parents at Sinai, and they promised God that they would keep his laws – a promise they would quickly forget.

🐸 **Adventure Reading:**
  • Joshua says goodbye: **Joshua 24:28-33**

Joshua's resting place

Timnath Serah

Beth Horon

Azekah

Lachish

Eglon

Makkedah

Debir

58

THE LAND

In America, people can own a piece of land. In Israel that wasn't true. God owned all the land. You could say that God "loaned" the land to Israelites.

When Joshua divided the land among the tribes and families, each family in each tribe (except the tribe of Levi) received a piece of land. The family couldn't sell the land – it could only be inherited so that that piece of land would stay in that family forever. The land also couldn't be divided into smaller pieces.

For example, a father could not divide his land among two or three sons; all the land had to go to the oldest son.

But because the land belonged to God, God also said that if the Israelites did not obey him, he would take the land away from them – which is what happened not too many centuries later.

Fight! Fight! Fight!

Mt. Ebal

Covenant Renewal

Shechem

Mt. Gerizim

Bethel

Help!

Ai

Hey you!

Jericho

Plains of Moab

Gibeon

Valley of Achor

Abel Shittim

Jarmulth

(The Five Kings)

Boy, the Israelites sure fought a lot.

Yeah, they're worse than me and my brothers!

Dead Sea

Hebron

The Judges

After Joshua died, a sad time began. The twelve tribes were living in different parts of the country, and each tribe had its own leaders, but nobody was in charge of everybody.

The book of Judges says, "In those days Israel had no king; everyone did as he saw fit." The people began to forget God and disobey the laws he had given them. And so God would send armies from other nations around Israel to punish the Israelites.

Then, when the Israelites couldn't take it any longer, they remembered God and what he had told them. They prayed to God and asked him to deliver them from their enemies.

Yikes!

Head for the hills!

Sign

Well, at least the boys are enjoying themselves.

On the double, Private Chip!

Yes, sir!

Charge!

God listened and made one of the people a leader (called a "judge") who, with God's help, defeated the enemies, so that once again the people had peace.

But very soon the people forgot the lesson they had learned, and the same thing started all over again: The people forgot God, God sent enemies to make their life miserable, the people cried out to God, and God called someone else to be a leader (judge) to defeat the enemy.

It happened over and over again – at least twelve times. *Judges 2:6-3:4*

Originally swords were like sickles, used for slashing at enemies rather than thrusting at them.

Ehud

The strangest story in the book of Judges is the story of Judge Ehud. Eglon, the king of Moab, made life difficult for the Israelites. The Israelites had to pay Eglon a lot of money each year, and one year Ehud took the money to Eglon.

Before the guards allowed Ehud to see the king, they searched him for weapons but didn't find any. Ehud told the king, who was very fat, that he had a secret message for him, so the king sent all his servants away. When Eglon and Ehud were alone, Ehud stabbed the king with a sword.

Then Ehud locked the room where the dead king was and walked out of the palace through another door. After a while the servants began to wonder why it took so long for Ehud to give his message to the king. At first they thought that the king had gone to the bathroom, but finally they got worried and broke the door down, only to find the king dead.

How could they have missed the sword when they searched Ehud for weapons? They had only checked one side, but they didn't realize that Ehud was left-handed so that he carried his sword on the "wrong" side!

Judges 3:12-30

In many ancient societies, left-handed people were considered evil and were usually not given positions of authority.

OK, men, get ready – here they come!

Check out this strange stone carving! It was found in the hills of South Dakota. (We threw in this photo to see if you're still awake. Are you?)

By Baal, attack!

Deborah

One of the judges was a woman named Deborah. The Israelites had once again forgotten God, and God allowed the Canaanites to make life very difficult for them for twenty years.

Then God told Deborah to send for a man named Barak. Barak came with 10,000 soldiers, but he was afraid to go up against the Canaanites by himself – he would go only if Deborah came along. Deborah came along, but she told Barak that because he had been a coward, God would let a woman kill Sisera, the Canaanite general. And that's what happened. Barak defeated the Canaanites, but a woman named Jael managed to get it through Sisera's head that he was no longer welcome. *Judges 4:1-24*

BONK!

In the name of the Lord, **charge!**

Ebubulah, we're stuck!

Yes, ma'am, General Deborah. Right away!

BAFF!

BIFF!

Take that, you dirty Canaanite!

Shh! Shh! OK...1, 2,...

3! By George, **attack!**

No, no. That's not it. Try again.

1, 2, 3! By Baal, **attack!**

We forgot to pray again!

Madam, please! This is men's work!

Canaanite weapons from the time of the Judges. The dagger handle is bronze and the blade is iron. I have no idea what the chain is for – maybe a belt buckle for holding up Philistine pants?

No society in ancient times believed in the equality of men and women; it was very unusual for Deborah to be a leader.

Gideon

This time the Midianites had taken over the country, and the Israelites were left with nothing to eat. They sometimes even had to live in caves. Then God told Gideon that he would be the one to defeat the Midianites. Gideon didn't really want to be a judge, so he wanted to make very sure that he wasn't dreaming.

Gideon asked for a sign from God. He put a sheepskin on the ground and asked God to let the sheepskin be wet with dew in the morning, but not the ground around it. And when that happened, he still wasn't ready, so he asked God to do the opposite the next morning. And sure enough, the ground was wet with dew, but the sheepskin was dry.

A sword for the Lord and for Gideon!

The Midianites used camels in battle because they knew that horses dislike the smell of camels so much that they will not charge at them.

We're trying to get some sleep, for crying out loud!

Hey, why aren't you girls joining us?

Maybe later, Jay.

Let's get the control box from Chip.

Gideon started out with 32,000 soldiers. But God thought it was too many and said that anybody who was scared could go home – so 22,000 men left, and Gideon had only 10,000 soldiers.

But God said that that was still too many. Gideon took them to the water, and everybody drank on their knees – all except 300 men, who "lapped the water with their tongue like a dog." Gideon could take only those 300 men to defeat the army of the Midianites!

The Midianite army was sound asleep when Gideon and his 300 men quietly surrounded the camp, each man with a trumpet and a torch inside a jar. At Gideon's signal they all blew their trumpets and broke the jars so that the Midianites could see the torches, and it looked and sounded like the camp was surrounded by a large army.

The sudden noise confused the Midianites. They ran into each other and began killing each other! The Midianites who were still alive ran away as fast as they could.

And the land had peace again. 🐸 *Judges 6:1-7:24*

By any pagan god, **attack!**

Please, Lord, send us another judge!

Not again!

Samson

Before Samson was born, God told his mother that her baby would be special. He would become a judge and deliver Israel from the Philistines, who lived along the coast of the Mediterranean Sea. But, God said, he must never drink wine and he must never cut his hair.

Samson grew up to be a very strong man because God was with him. Once he even killed a lion with his bare hands. But one day he saw a Philistine woman and he wanted to marry her, even though God had said very clearly that no Israelite should ever marry anyone from another nation. And that certainly included the Philistines, Israel's enemies.

Samson never married her, because the Philistines tricked him. But he got so mad at the Philistines that he killed thirty of them.

BOFF!

BIFF!

BAFF!

1002 Take a number

Q: How long did Samson love Delilah?

Later, Samson met another Philistine woman, Delilah. Delilah got Samson to tell her that if his hair was cut off, he would lose his strength. So Delilah cut Samson's hair, and the Philistines were finally able to overpower Samson. They stabbed his eyes out and took him to the temple of Dagon, their main god.

Samson stood in the middle of the temple, between the two pillars that supported the roof. There were about 3,000 people in the temple when Samson prayed that God would give him his strength back one last time. God answered Samson's prayer. Samson pushed against the pillars and the temple came crashing down on the people who were there, including Samson.

Judges 13:1-16:31

Hey!

Thanks!

A: Until she bald him out.

Gates were the weakest point in the wall, so they had to be very big and heavy. Samson carried gates like these on his shoulders (Judges 16:3)!

At the end of the book of Judges, things weren't much better than they had been at the beginning: "In those days Israel had no king; everyone did as he saw fit." *Judges 21:25*

Ruth

During the time of the judges, good things happened as well. One of those is the beautiful story of Ruth and Boaz.

A man from Bethlehem took his family to Moab because there was a famine in Israel. (Remember, the Moabites were Israel's enemies – Ehud had killed Eglon, the king of Moab.)

The man's two sons married Moabite women (which they weren't supposed to – Israelites should not marry foreigners). But then the man died, and his two sons died as well, so that the man's wife, Naomi, was left alone in Moab with her two daughters-in-law, Ruth and Orpah.

Naomi decided to go back to Bethlehem. Ruth went with her because she loved Naomi and trusted God.

To understand what happened next, remember how important it was that the land stayed in the same family. If a man died without having any children who could inherit his land, his widow had to marry his closest relative (his brother, or if he didn't have a brother, a cousin). Then, when the widow had children, they would be considered the children of the man who had died and they could inherit his land. This relative who married the widow was called the "kinsman-redeemer."

66

Naomi remembered that her husband had a relative called Boaz, who was a rich farmer. So Naomi told Ruth to go to Boaz's fields and pick up grain behind the harvesters. (God's law provided for the poor people in Israel by telling farmers that when they harvested they had to leave some grain behind that could be picked up by any poor person.)

When Boaz found out that Ruth was the widow of a relative, he obeyed God's law. He knew that there was a closer relative, so he first gave that man the opportunity to take over the land and to marry Ruth.

But Boaz liked Ruth, and he told the man, "If you don't want to marry her, I'll do it."

The other man refused to marry Ruth, and he handed one of his sandals to Boaz. This was a very old custom that meant the same thing as our signing a contract. The custom was so old that when the book of Ruth was written people didn't remember it, so there is an explanation right in the middle of the story (Ruth 4:7).

Boaz obeyed God and married Ruth. And because of Ruth's faith and love and Boaz's obedience, their great-grandson would be King David, the greatest king Israel ever had. More than a thousand years later, the Lord Jesus would be born in Bethlehem from the family of David.

Ruth 1-4 (the whole book!)

Oprah Winfrey's name came from a misspelling of the biblical name "Orpah" on her birth certificate.

Samuel

1 Samuel

The tabernacle, where the Israelites worshiped God, had been built in the wilderness by Moses. When the Israelites conquered Canaan, the tabernacle had been put in Shiloh, in the territory of Ephraim. And there it stayed for almost 200 years.

At Shiloh the last (and the greatest) of the judges lived: Samuel.

Before Samuel was born, his mother, Hannah, had not been able to have children. The Israelites thought that if a woman could not have children, God was punishing her. But Hannah came to the tabernacle with her husband every year, as God had told all Israelites to do, and one year she cried and prayed to God to give her a son. She promised that if God gave her a son, she would give him to the Lord.

Mary, the mother of Jesus, wrote a song (Luke 1:46-55) that is very similar to the song that Hannah wrote (1 Samuel 2:1-10).

This model of the tabernacle shows the walls and everything inside covered with gold. Behind the curtain is the Most Holy Place, where the ark stood.

ONE HOUR LATER

Outta sight, man!

Groovy afro!

Far out!

Rebecca! What's with the tie dye and bell bottoms?

What a trip!

Eli, the priest in charge of the tabernacle, saw Hannah praying and thought that she was drunk. When Eli realized that she wasn't drunk at all but very upset because she couldn't have children, he told her that God would give her a son. And even though Eli was not a very good priest, he was right.

The next year Hannah did have a son, and she called him Samuel (which means "Asked of God"). When Samuel was old enough, Hannah took him to the tabernacle, where he became Eli's helper. 🐸 *1 Samuel 1:1-28*

One night, when Samuel was barely a teenager, he heard someone call him. Samuel went to Eli to see why he had called, but Eli hadn't called at all. Again the voice called Samuel, and again it wasn't Eli. When the same thing happened a third time, Eli realized that it was God himself who was calling Samuel.

The next time Samuel heard the voice, he said, "Speak, for your servant is listening." And God told Samuel that he would punish Eli and his family because Eli's sons disobeyed God's laws and Eli had done nothing to keep his sons in line.
🐸 *1 Samuel 3:1-21*

One day, the Israelites decided to fight the Philistines. They took with them the ark from the tabernacle, as if the ark were a mascot. They didn't trust God – they trusted the ark!

Of course the Philistines defeated the Israelites and took the ark with them. Eli's sons were killed in the battle, and when Eli heard that the ark had been captured, he fell backward off his chair and broke his neck and died. 🐸 *1 Samuel 4:1-18*

The Philistines took the ark to Ashdod, to the temple of their god Dagon, and put it beside the statue of Dagon. But the next morning the statue had fallen on its face before the ark! The Philistines put the statue back in place, but the next morning it had fallen again, and its head and hands had broken off and were lying by the door.

And strange things happened to the people of Ashdod as long as the ark was there – God sent swarms of rats, and the people all got very sick. Finally the Philistines took the ark to a different city, but the same things happened there.

And the people of a third city did not even want the ark after they heard what had happened in the first two cities, so the ark was sent back to Israel. The Philistines even sent gifts with the ark: rats and tumors made of gold!

The ark never returned to the tabernacle. The Israelites took it to the village of Kiriath Jearim, where it stayed for twenty years.
1 Samuel 5:1-12; 6:10-12; 6:21-7:1

Samuel became Israel's leader. But he was different from all the other judges, who had been only military leaders; Samuel was also a prophet.

Under Samuel's leadership the Israelites decided that they wanted to follow God after all. They all came together in Mizpah, and Samuel prayed for them.

But the Philistines thought that the Israelites were getting together to fight with them, and they decided to attack first. The Israelites were afraid, but God sent loud thunder that made the Philistines even more scared than the Israelites already were, and the Philistines ran off. *1 Samuel 7:7-11*

Philistines

The Philistines lived along the shore of the Mediterranean Sea. They had five cities: Ashdod, Ashkelon, Gath, Ekron, and Gaza (today in Israel there is still an area called the Gaza Strip).

The Philistines gave the Israelites all kinds of problems during the first few centuries the Israelites lived in Canaan.

Before the Israelites had a king, they found it very hard to fight the Philistines, who were much better organized and who had another great advantage: their weapons were made of iron and were much harder than the bronze weapons of the Israelites. (Bronze is a mixture of copper and tin.)

Before David became king, he lived with the Philistines for a while and learned how they planned wars, so that when he became king, David could defeat the Philistines once and for all.

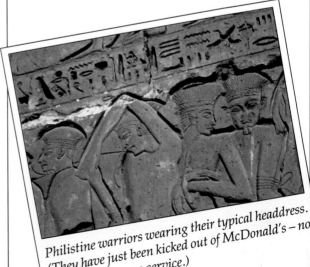

Philistine warriors wearing their typical headdress. (They have just been kicked out of McDonald's – no shirt, no shoes, no service.)

Ancient history is divided into three main periods, based on the type of materials used for tools and weapons: the Stone Age, the Bronze Age, and the Iron Age.

Abraham and Moses lived in the Bronze Age, and David lived in the Iron Age.

Saul

1 Samuel

When Samuel was old, he wanted to make his sons judges over Israel. But Samuel's sons weren't any better than Eli's sons had been. They were more interested in making money by taking bribes than in obeying God.

The elders of Israel came to Samuel and said, "Look, we need a king like all the nations around us to keep us together!"

When Samuel asked God about it, God said, "They are really rejecting me as their king – and they have done so ever since they left Egypt!" God told Samuel to warn the Israelites that if they got a king like they wanted, their king would not make life easy for them. He would make the people pay taxes and force their sons to serve in the army, and the people would become servants of the king. *1 Samuel 8:1-22*

But the people wanted a king anyway. God chose Saul, from the tribe of Benjamin (the smallest of the tribes), to be the first king. Samuel told Saul that he would be Israel's first king, and he "anointed" Saul by putting some oil on his forehead.

Saul certainly looked like a king. He was an impressive man, a head taller than the rest of the Israelites. When the Israelites came together to choose a king, they cast lots (somewhat like our drawing straws, except that the Israelites used stones of different shapes and colors). They trusted God to guide the lots so that the right man would be chosen.

When Saul was finally chosen, no one could find him – he was hiding among the baggage! *1 Samuel 9:1-10:1; 10:17-27*

This has gone far enough.

I hope you girls are having fun!

Lighten up, Jay! Clowns are supposed to smile!

Yeah, Bozo. For our next blitz we'll go to something more natural.

I hope the guys on my team never hear about this!

LONG LIVE KING SAUL

72

At first, Saul not only looked like a king but also acted like one. He defeated the Ammonites, and the people loved him. But Saul didn't turn out to be the kind of king everybody thought he would be. One day, the Israelites attacked the Amalekites. Samuel had told Saul that God wanted the Israelites to destroy completely the Amalekites and anything that belonged to them – including all their cattle.

Sigh. Isn't he dreamy?

Long live King Saul!

In most societies around Israel, the king was considered to be a god.

Saul disobeyed. He saved the best of the Amalekites' sheep and cattle for himself and then pretended that he had saved them to sacrifice them to the Lord – even though the Lord had told him to kill them all.

It didn't seem to be a big thing, but Samuel told Saul that he would be replaced as king because he had not obeyed God. God wants obedience more than sacrifices! From that point on Saul's life went downhill, until in the end he killed himself.

1 Samuel 15:1-34

David

1 Samuel

After Saul disobeyed God, God sent Samuel to Bethlehem, to the house of Jesse, to anoint the next king. God didn't choose one of Jesse's seven grown-up sons but his youngest son, David, who was a shepherd.

In the meantime, Saul's life went from bad to worse. He became very depressed and angry – the Bible says "an evil spirit tormented him." One thing that made Saul feel better was music. Saul heard that David played the harp very well, so he invited David to come to the palace. David played for Saul whenever the king was feeling terrible, and Saul would cheer up a bit. Saul liked David, but he didn't know yet that David would soon take his place as king! 🐸 *1 Samuel 16:1-23*

Clay figurines like this lute player were used for oil jars, lamps, or perfume bottles. (Maybe this is an early Precious Moments figurine!)

I can't bear it.

You ain't lyin'.

Q: What dishonest instrument did David play? A: The lyre.

We're slammin'!

David had a little lamb, little lamb, little lamb, David had a little lamb with fleece as white as snow.

Grumble. All those costume changes are messing up the molecular configuration of our holographic figures...

Baa-ad joke, girls.

I was trying to program a back-to-nature look. You know, all-natural fibers?

Where's my Woolite?

What Is "Anointing"?

In Old Testament times, oil was very important. It was used, for example, for cooking and for lamps. It was also used to anoint people (and sometimes things). "Anointing" means to put oil on someone (or something).

Most kinds of anointing were nothing special. Oil was put on wounds to make them heal, and rubbed on skin and hair to make them shiny. And since people didn't take a bath very often in those days, they used scented oil to make them smell better.

But there was also a special and very important kind of anointing. When God chose someone to do a special job, that person was anointed. In the Old Testament, three kinds of people were anointed: kings, priests, and prophets.

- Priests spoke to God on behalf of the people;
- Prophets spoke to the people on behalf of God;
- Kings ruled over the people as God's representatives.

Lions prowled Palestine until A.D. 1100. (Rumor has it they were beaten by the Chicago Bears.)

Houston: We have liftoff.

Blitz activated.

Good King Saul was a merry old soul, and a merry old soul was he.

He sent for his harp and he sent for his pipe and he sent for his fiddlers three!

75

David & Goliath

One day, when David had gone back to taking care of his father's sheep, the Philistines were bothering Israel again. The Philistine army and the army of the Israelites were sitting across from each other on two hills, ready to fight.

But the Philistines didn't want to fight in the usual way. They had a secret weapon: Goliath. Goliath was more than nine feet tall, and his armor weighed a whopping 125 pounds.

Goliath stepped out into the valley and yelled at the Israelites, "You guys send someone down here to fight with me. If I kill him, you surrender to us; if your guy kills me, our army surrenders to you!"

Of course, Goliath knew that nobody could beat him, and the Israelites were getting more and more frustrated because Goliath kept yelling at them. But no one from the Israelite army stepped forward to fight.

Then David came to visit his brothers who were in the army. David heard Goliath and he knew that he had to do something. Saul didn't want David to fight with Goliath, but David told him that he had killed lions and bears to protect his sheep. So Saul had his men put armor on David, but David couldn't move with the armor on and decided to go in his regular clothes – knowing that God was on his side!

When Goliath saw David, he was furious because David was only a boy. Goliath cursed and yelled, but when he attacked, David didn't run away – he ran toward Goliath. And while he was running he put a stone in his slingshot and hurled the stone at Goliath. It hit Goliath in the only place that was not protected: his forehead. Goliath fell down, unconscious. And then David killed Goliath with the giant's own sword. Suddenly the young shepherd was a national hero. Saul made David an officer in the army, and David was successful every time Saul sent him and his soldiers out to fight a battle. The people loved David – in fact, David became more popular than Saul, and Saul became very jealous of David. 🐸 1 Samuel 17:1-58

LOOK OUT!

Was that Goliath or the Jolly Green Giant?

Either that or Peter Pan has been taking a truckload of vitamins.

Hey, Chip. Where'd you get the input for Goliath?

Ah, um…a television commercial.

The more popular David became, the more jealous and angry Saul got. Finally it got so bad that Saul wanted to kill David, and David had to hide in caves in the wilderness of Judah. *1 Samuel 18:1-16*

God had told David that he would be king, but here he was, hunted like an animal. David often wondered why he had to go through all this.

Adventure readings:
- The friendship of David and Jonathan;
  1 Samuel 20:1-42
- David refuses to kill Saul;
  1 Samuel 24:1-22

Some people think that the book of Job is the oldest book in the Bible. That means that David may actually have read it – and he would have understood it, because Job talks about the very difficult question, Why do bad things happen to good people? And that was exactly the question David was asking.

I can't believe the girls dressed me as a bunny.

Don't worry. I've got a plan to get back at them. Listen... psst psst psst psst.

David sure had a rough time.

Do you suppose God planned it all?

I don't know, but he sure used it to make David strong!

78

Job

Job was a rich man who loved God. But suddenly, in one day, he lost everything – his house, his children, his possessions, and finally his health. Job sat on the garbage pile, scratching his itching sores. He couldn't understand why such terrible things happened to him.

(The first two chapters of the book of Job explain that all these awful things had not happened because Job had done anything bad. But Job never knew that part of the story.)

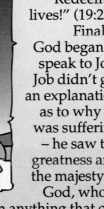

When Job's friends, Eliphaz, Bildad, and Zophar, heard what had happened to Job, they came to see him.
🐸 *Job 1:1-2:13*

The first thing Job said was, "I wish I had never been born! I wish I were dead!"
🐸 *Job 3:1-26*

Job's friends told him that he must have done something terrible to deserve all this. But Job knew that that wasn't true.

The more Job said so, the more his friends kept telling him that it *had* to be true.
🐸 *Job 11:14-20*

Job cried out, "Isn't there anyone who can speak to God on my behalf?" (9:32-33). He wondered why God let him suffer, and he even was angry with God. But Job never rejected God. Even when he suffered terribly, he still trusted God and said, "I know that my Redeemer lives!" (19:25). Finally, God began to speak to Job. Job didn't get an explanation as to why he was suffering – he saw the greatness and the majesty of God, who is greater than anything that can happen to us. 🐸 *Job 38:1-21*

In the end, God gave Job his health back and he became a rich man again. (God was mad at Job's three friends, though, because they accused Job without knowing what they were talking about.)
🐸 *Job 42:7-17*

Job probably lived around the time of Abraham.

King David

2 Samuel

Saul made life difficult for David, but not for long. Saul killed himself on the battle field, and soon after that David became king, first of the tribes of Judah and Benjamin, and then of all the Israelites. ➤ *1 Samuel 31:1-5*

❧ **Adventure reading:**
• Saul and the witch of Endor;
1 Samuel 28:1-25

David was king of the Israelites, but there was one city right in the center of his kingdom he hadn't captured yet: Jerusalem (or, as it was then still called, Jebus, where the Jebusites lived).

Back then, the city was still small but very difficult to capture because it was built on a rock that stuck out from the hillside, with valleys on three sides.

David's soldiers entered the city by crawling up through a water shaft that went down from the city into the valley. David made Jebus his capital and called it Jerusalem, which means "City of Peace." ➤ *2 Samuel 5:1-12*

One of the first things David did after he captured Jerusalem was to bring the ark of the covenant to Jerusalem from the village of Kiriath Jearim where it had been stored ever since the Philistines brought it back to Israel.

David built a temporary shelter for the ark. He wanted to build a temple for God so that the ark would have a proper home, but God told David that he couldn't build the temple but that his son would build it. All David could do was collect materials for the building of the temple.

80

There was a big celebration when the ark was brought to Jerusalem, with music and singing. David was so excited that he danced in front of the ark. (David's wife was a bit stuffy and didn't approve of David's dancing in public.)
2 Samuel 6:1-23

Adventure reading:

• God's promises to David: **2 Samuel 7:11b-16**

All right. Who messed up the layout here?

Jerusalem is about 3,800 years old – much older than the Bible's first mention of it.

David was 37 when he conquered the city of Jerusalem.

Three of the world's largest religions – Judaism, Christianity, and Islam – all consider Jerusalem to be a holy city.

LONG LIVE KING ~~SAUL~~ DAVID

avid wrote many beautiful songs. We still have many of those songs in the book of Psalms. We don't have any idea what the melodies were or how the psalms may have sounded. There are musical instructions at the beginning of several psalms, for example, Psalm 53, but we don't know what most of them mean. We do know that they must have sounded beautiful because they were sung from the heart.

Psalms

Singing has always been an important part of worshiping God. The Israelites loved to sing, and they had a marvelous songbook: the book of Psalms.

There are many different kinds of psalms. If people were happy, they could sing praise songs. If they were sick, they could express their worry to God in a psalm. If they were feeling guilty because of something they did, they could use a psalm to confess their sins to God. And they could even use a psalm to express anger at God.

The Psalms were written by a number of people. For example, Psalm 90 was written by Moses. Psalms 72 and 127 were written by David's son, King Solomon. But more than half of the psalms were written by King David (76 to be exact).

Many of the psalms are not only songs but also prayers. The psalms express all kinds of feelings, and a psalm can say exactly what you feel. For example,

- If, like the Israelites, you want to praise God, read Psalm 19 or Psalm 103 or Psalm 150.
- If you want to tell God that you trust him and his love for you, read Psalm 37.
- If you are grateful, read Psalm 100 or Psalm 136.
- If you want to tell God you're sorry about doing something bad, read Psalm 32 or Psalm 51.
- If you are sad, read Psalm 130 or Psalm 131.
- If you just want to think about God's goodness, read Psalm 23.

There are also psalms that talk about the coming of Jesus, the Messiah: Psalm 2 and Psalm 22.

And there are psalms that sing about God's faithfulness in the past that shows that we can trust him today: Psalm 106 and Psalm 136.

When you read or sing or pray the Psalms, you know that there have been millions of people who have read and sung and prayed these very same psalms before you for thousands of years!

David & Bathsheba
2 Samuel

David was king, but Israel still had many enemies, such as the Philistines, Moabites, Edomites, and Ammonites. The first years of David's kingship were years of fighting and war.

God had promised to give David the kingdom, but when God makes a promise it doesn't mean that we can just sit back and wait for things to happen.

David defeated all the enemies with God's help. His kingdom now was large and strong, and the nations around Israel no longer even thought about attacking David. Jerusalem was really becoming a "city of peace."

One day, David didn't go out to fight at the head of his army as usual. His generals were able to handle the war, and they knew that if David was killed in battle the kingdom would fall apart again. So David stayed home and his soldiers went out to fight.

While the army was fighting, David was taking it easy on the roof of his palace one evening (all buildings had flat roofs back then) when he saw a beautiful woman down below. David decided then and there that he wanted to marry her.

The problem was that the woman, Bathsheba, was already married to Uriah, a soldier in the army. David solved the problem by doing something terrible. David, the king who had been blessed by God and who (as we see in the psalms he wrote) loved God, decided to get rid of Bathsheba's husband.

He told the army commander to put Uriah at the very front of the army in the next battle so that Uriah would have a good chance of being killed. And that's exactly what happened.

2 Samuel 11:1-27

Four women are listed in Matthew's record of Jesus' ancestors in Matthew 1: Tamar, Rahab, Ruth, and Bathsheba.

I'm not landing on my head. I'm not landing on my head...

Now David could marry Bathsheba. But God sent a prophet named Nathan, who told David a parable about a rich man who stole the only sheep from a poor man. When David got angry about such injustice, Nathan said, "You are the man who did this when you took Bathsheba from Uriah!"

Every sin has bad results. After David's sin with Bathsheba God told David, "The sword will never depart from your house," meaning that there would always be fighting and turmoil in David's own family and in his kingdom. How true that turned out to be!

David told God he was very, very sorry. He meant it with all his heart. He asked for forgiveness, and God forgave him. 🐸 *2 Samuel 12:1-14*
🐸 *Psalm 51 (David's prayer for forgiveness)*

Sorry, gang. RAM overload. Is everyone OK? We won't go on any more camel rides, OK, Brad?

DEAD SEA

Chip! Wait till I get my hands on you!

THE RED SEA

Bows and arrows are among the earliest known weapons. With a good bow, arrows could be shot as far as 400 yards. (The length of four football fields without the end zones.)

85

David & Absalom

2 Samuel

What strange thing did Absalom do to steal the hearts of the people? See 2 Samuel 15:5-6.

God's warning that there would always be fighting in David's family came true very soon. David had many sons (he also had quite a few wives, as was usual in those days). One of his sons was Absalom, who decided that he wanted to be king. Absalom did his very best to get rid of his father. It broke David's heart to see his son, whom he loved very much, trying to fight him.

Absalom's army lost the fight with David's army, and Absalom had to run for his life. He tried to escape on a mule (a cross between a horse and a donkey). The mule ran underneath a tree, and Absalom forgot to duck. His long hair got tangled in a branch, and there was Absalom, hanging by his hair, while the mule kept going. That's how David's army commander found him and that's where he killed Absalom.

Where are we?

Must be a model of Solomon's temple.

Solomon built his temple on the exact spot where Abraham nearly sacrificed his son, Isaac.

When David heard what had happened to Absalom he cried and mourned a long time. In spite of all the bad things Absalom had done to him, David still loved his son. *2 Samuel 18:5-17; 19:4*

David knew that there were quite a few people who would like to be king after he died. So, when he was getting old, David made sure that everybody knew who would be king after he died: Solomon, the son of David and Bathsheba. David asked the leaders of Israel to make sure that the kingdom would stay together after his death by helping Solomon.

David also showed the leaders the plans for the temple that Solomon would build in Jerusalem, and he told them about all the building materials for the temple that he had collected. David also asked the leaders to give money for the new temple, and they gave gladly.

The young shepherd who became a hero when he killed Goliath died as the king over a strong nation – but more important than that, he died as a man who, even though he sinned during his life, loved God.

Solomon

1 Kings

Maybe now I'll make the basketball team!

Chip, why couldn't you do this when we met up with the jolly green Goliath?

Solomon became king. He was smart – so smart that he knew how easy it is to make mistakes and do unwise things. So when God told Solomon that he would give him whatever he asked for, Solomon did not ask for money or power – he asked for wisdom. And God gave Solomon great wisdom. *1 Kings 3:1-28*

For example, one day two women came to Solomon. Each had a baby, but one of the babies had died, and now both women wanted the other baby. They both said the same thing: "It's my baby!" Solomon found a simple solution: He said, "Let's cut the baby in half, so you can each have half a baby." One of the women thought it was a good idea, but the real mother, who of course loved her baby, said, "No! Give it to the other woman, but don't hurt my baby!" So Solomon knew who the real mother was. *1 Kings 4:29-34*

One of the greatest Greek wise men said, "Know yourself." Solomon said, "Know God."

Archaeologists would love to excavate the area of Solomon's temple, but Muslims have built a mosque there (see photo on page 156), and they will not permit any digging.

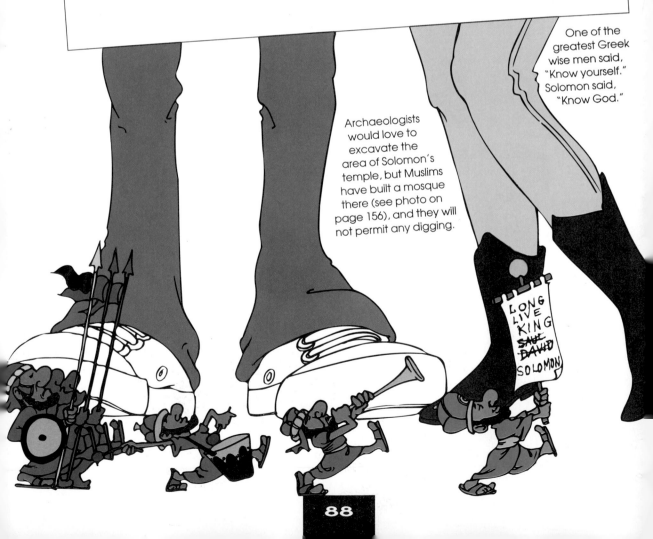

LONG LIVE KING ~~SAUL~~ ~~DAVID~~ SOLOMON

Let me adjust the magnification and let's do the blitz. Ready, wise guys?

Just call me Mt. Rebecca, elevation 5,200 feet. If I had dandruff, I'd be a ski slope!

You're sure head and shoulders above the rest.

These are what's left of the cedars of Lebanon. They wouldn't even make good Christmas trees. The cedars used to build Solomon's temple were much larger, like our redwood trees.

Solomon had asked for wisdom instead of riches. God gave him wisdom, but Solomon also became very rich. He used his wisdom to make good business deals – buying, selling, and trading.

The greatest thing Solomon did was to build the temple. David had made the plans, but Solomon actually built it, or rather, he drafted 30,000 men from all over Israel and they built the temple.

The king of Tyre in Lebanon, north of Israel, agreed to sell Solomon all the cedar and pine wood he needed for the temple and for other buildings. Back in Solomon's time the cedars of Lebanon were famous. They were tall and straight and beautiful. Since then, almost all the trees have been cut down, and the country now looks very different.

It took seven years to build the temple, but it was worth it. It was a beautiful building that stood for almost 500 years. It was the house of God, the place where the Israelites worshiped God, who had delivered them from Egypt and who had given them a country to live in. In the temple, in the Most Holy Place, was the ark of the covenant, with the two large stones on which God himself had written the Ten Commandments.

1 Kings 5:1-6:38

Proverbs

Solomon, like his father David, was a writer. He wrote psalms (Psalm 72 and Psalm 127), and he wrote many proverbs.

A proverb is a short statement that says in a few words something that is usually true about life. For example, "Haste makes waste" and "The early bird catches the worm" are American proverbs that people have been using for a long time. You could say that a proverb is a whole sermon in one sentence.

Most of the proverbs in the book of Proverbs were written by King Solomon, but they were collected and put into the book of Proverbs about 250 years later by one of King Solomon's descendants, King Hezekiah.

The book of Proverbs is very practical. It talks about things that are part of everybody's life: work, honesty, living with your neighbors (which includes brothers and sisters!), not being proud, being a good son or daughter, being a good parent, and many more things.

The book of Proverbs is the kind of book you read a little bit at a time and then think about what it says and what it would mean if you did (or did not) do what it says.

Step right up to the Circus of Life! Be a rich man, be a poor man, be a wise man, be a fool — only two bucks a role! Just lay your cash down here, close the book, and I'll let you in! Trust me!

A friend loves at all times. (Proverbs 17:17)

The lips of the wise spread knowledge. (Proverbs 15:7)

Not so the hearts of fools! (Proverbs 15:7)

A chattering fool comes to ruin. (Proverbs 10:8)

How long will you lie there, you sluggard? (Proverbs 6:9)

Altogether, Solomon wrote 3,000 proverbs; not all of them are in the Bible (1 Kings 4:32).

CIRCUS of LIFE!

Dogs are mentioned forty-one times in the Bible, but cats aren't mentioned at all.

A penny saved is a penny earned.

Hey, that's not in Proverbs!

Yeah, Benjamin Franklin wrote that.

Here are just a few of the many things the book of Proverbs says:

You are wise if you
- listen to others (12:15)
- love someone who tells you when you are doing something wrong (9:7-8)
- save for the future (21:20)
- make your parents happy (29:3)

You are foolish if you
- idle away your time (12:11)
- don't listen to others (10:8)
- say bad things about other people (10:18)
- won't listen to your parents' advice (15:5)

You are a good friend if you
- are always loyal (17:17)
- never give up on your friends (27:10)
- overlook mistakes (17:9)

You are lazy if you
- sleep your life away (6:9)
- always have an excuse for yourself (22:13)
- would rather get than give (21:25-26)

You are successful if you
- trust God (28:25)
- obey God's Word (13:13)
- work hard (12:24)
- can admit mistakes and don't repeat them (28:13)

Solomon's Riches

1 Kings

Solomon liked to build things. He not only built the temple but also a palace for himself (which took thirteen years) and a palace for Pharaoh's daughter, who was his wife. And he built or repaired many cities throughout his kingdom.

For his building projects, Solomon used slave labor: people from other nations who lived in Israel or who had been made prisoners of war. The Israelites once had been slaves who had to build cities for the pharaoh of Egypt; now the king of the Israelites used people from other nations to build his cities.

To give you an idea of how many people lived and worked in Solomon's palace, here is what the people at the court ate every day: 560 bushels of flour and cornmeal, 30 cows, 100 sheep and goats, and numerous deer, gazelles, and birds.

1 Kings 4:20-28

This looks nothing like Solomon's palace, but Brad's little brother built it and we promised him we'd put it in our report.

A man can do nothing better than to eat and drink and find satisfaction in his work. (Ecclesiastes 2:24)

Under King Solomon's rule, Israel was a prosperous, peaceful country. Solomon became very famous, so famous that people in faraway countries heard about him. One of those people was the queen of Sheba, who decided that she wanted to visit Solomon and talk with him.

It was not just a trip she made on an afternoon when she had nothing better to do. Her country was probably somewhere in southern Arabia, some 1,200 miles from Jerusalem. It was a long camel ride across the hot desert, made dangerous by groups of bandits who would take any opportunity to rob the queen of the treasures she brought with her to give to Solomon.

Among those treasures were spices. To us it seems odd to give cinnamon or nutmeg to a king, but in those days only the very wealthy could afford them, and the queen of Sheba brought more spices for Solomon than had ever been brought before or would be brought into Israel until modern times. It was truly a royal gift!

She came not just because she was curious, but because she was looking for wisdom and understanding, and Solomon did not disappoint her. When she left to go back to Sheba, she praised the God of Israel for what he had done for his people. *1 Kings 10:1-13*

The nation of Sheba was involved in international trade; it brought valuable goods from India and Africa through the desert to Gaza and Damascus.

How Rich was Solomon?

To get an idea of Solomon's riches, read 1 Kings 10:14-29. You'll see that one of the things he received was gold – 666 talents every year. That is about 50,000 pounds of gold. Today that would be enough money to buy a ten-dollar pizza for every man, woman, and child in Alaska, Arizona, Colorado, Idaho, Montana, Nebraska, Nevada, New Mexico, North Dakota, Oregon, South Dakota, Utah, Washington, and Wyoming – with enough money left over for a big tip for the totally exhausted delivery person.

Wow! Have you ever seen so much money in your life?

Watch it, Jay. Remember: "Whoever loves money never has money enough." (Ecclesiastes 5:10)

Yummy! Dead flies! (Ecclesiastes 10:1)

One of the things that must have impressed the Queen of Sheba was Solomon's horses and chariots. He had so many – 12,000 horses and 4,000 chariots – that he built special cities around the country to house the horses and chariots, which could be dispatched quickly to defend the country against attack.

But even the wisest person can make mistakes – and Solomon made a BIG one. It began when he married the daughter of the pharaoh of Egypt, even though God had said that Israelites should not marry people from other countries.

Solomon had many, many wives – about 700 in all. Many of these wives were not Israelites, and they had brought the gods from their own countries with them and worshiped these idols. But the really sad thing was that when Solomon was old, he himself began to worship some of these idols, and he even built places where these idols could be worshiped.

The young king who had asked God for wisdom became an old man who made the greatest mistake of all: He turned away from God, who had given him everything. And God was angry. He told Solomon that after Solomon's death the great kingdom would be taken away from his family.

🐛 *1 Kings 11:1-14*

Solomon had had everything; he had done everything. But he found out that without God it was all meaningless and a waste of time. Toward the end of his life, Solomon wrote a sad book about how meaningless his life had become: the book of Ecclesiastes.

Megiddo was one of the cities Solomon built for his 12,000 horses. In the background you see the part of the tell that hasn't been dug up yet (see page 35).

Y'know, Chip, I don't know why, but I'm still hungry.

Of course. It's only a hollow gram!

Megiddo was the site of many battles; the book of Revelation prophesies that the final battle between good and evil will take place at Har Megiddo ("Mount Megiddo"), called Armageddon in Greek.

Ecclesiastes

Solomon (who calls himself the Teacher) begins by saying, "Meaningless! Meaningless! Everything is meaningless!" And he doesn't get much more cheerful in the rest of the book.

Ecclesiastes 1:1-14; 3:1-8

Why is this strange book in the Bible at all? Have you ever felt really empty inside and sad because things just didn't make much sense? The book of Ecclesiastes says exactly what many kids and adults sometimes feel: What's the use? Why get excited about anything if it doesn't make any difference in the long run anyway? For example, by the time we grow up, the earth will probably be ruined anyway!

God gave us the book of Ecclesiastes to let us know that we aren't the only ones who feel this way, and that when everything seems meaningless it really is not meaningless – God is still in charge! Sooner or later we all realize that

- Knowing a lot
- Studying hard
- Having a good time
- Working hard
- Making lots of money
- Trying to be the best at something

– none of these can make us happy forever. In the long run they are meaningless.

But in the end, King Solomon says, there are two things in life that are really important: To fear God (to "fear" God does not mean to be afraid of him but to trust and love him with awe and reverence) and to obey his commandments (Ecclesiastes 12:13).

Ecclesiastes 12:1, 9-14

Ecclesiastes is a Greek word meaning "preacher" or "teacher."

Hey, Brad, Solomon says: "All man's efforts are for his mouth, yet his appetite is never satisfied!" (Ecclesiastes 6:7)

OK, that's enough Solomonizing for one day.

I can't believe I ate the whole thing!

The Song of Songs (which means "the greatest song ever") is only one of 1,005 songs that Solomon composed during his lifetime (1 Kings 4:32).

Song of Songs

Solomon wrote yet another book, which is very different from Ecclesiastes. It is a beautiful love poem, which he probably wrote when he was still a young king: the Song of Songs.

We use the word *love* a lot. "I love my mom and dad"; "I love my sister (sometimes)"; "I love pizza"; "I love recess"; "I love my dog." The word *love* means something a little bit different in each of these sentences (if it didn't, you could end up hugging your pizza and eating your dog).

But there is yet another, special kind of love – the love that a man and a woman have for each other that leads to marriage. The Song of Songs is a love song that doesn't even talk about God. It is in the Bible because God wants to tell us that the love between a man and a woman is something very beautiful. God cares not just about "spiritual" things but about everything that is important in people's lives.

When people are in love they sometimes say things to each other that sound kind of mushy or strange to everybody else. Listen to what Solomon says to his fiancée: "Your eyes are like doves and your hair is like a flock of goats" (Song of Songs 4:1). The amazing thing is that she actually likes what Solomon says, because she knows that Solomon is telling her that he loves her.

God loves us even more than Solomon loved his bride. People who don't know God often think that the Bible is a strange book and that it is silly to read it. But when you know that God loves you, it makes sense to read the Bible because it tells you in many ways how much God really loves you! *Song of Songs 2:1-17*

Who's that? Mr. and Mrs. Frank N. Stein?

Hey, Chip, what's next? Have you got the magnification under control? What about Max? Why does he keep coming back? Can't you get rid of him? How about if you let me try?

Um…well…

When Solomon died, he had been king for forty years. They had been good years. But they were the last years of peace and prosperity the country ever saw.

According to an old Jewish saying, people should not read the Song of Songs until they are thirty years old. (That's a PG30 rating!)

The Divided Kingdom

1 Kings

After Solomon died, his son Rehoboam became king. He inherited his father's kingdom, but he didn't inherit any of his father's wisdom.

Solomon's building projects had cost a lot of money, and in the last years when Solomon was king the people of Israel had had to pay heavy taxes. As soon as Rehoboam became king, the people begged him to let them pay less taxes.

Rehoboam asked the older men, who in the past had given advice to his father, what he should do. They told him he should give the people what they asked for and lower their taxes.

But Rehoboam's friends, who were still young, told him that he should ask for even more money from the people, and Rehoboam listened to his friends.

When he told the people that they would have to pay even more, the ten tribes in the northern part of Israel decided that they had had enough. They formed their own kingdom, and they chose Jeroboam to be their king.

God's warning to Solomon had come true: The great kingdom of David and Solomon was now divided into two small, much weaker kingdoms. The northern kingdom was called Israel. Only two tribes, Judah and Benjamin, were left in what was now the southern kingdom; it was called Judah.

God had told David that his house would fight against itself, and it came true: The two kingdoms often fought with each other.

In ancient societies, a new king was usually the oldest son of the previous king.

Mediterranean Sea

Welcome to Israel the Northern Kingdom

Leaving Judah, the Southern Kingdom. Ya'll come back!

Bethel •

Reuben
Simeon
Issachar
Zebulun
Gad
Asher
Dan
Naphtali
Ephraim
Manasseh

Jerusalem •

Benjamin
Judah

Dead Sea

OK, Jay. If you can do better, go right ahead.

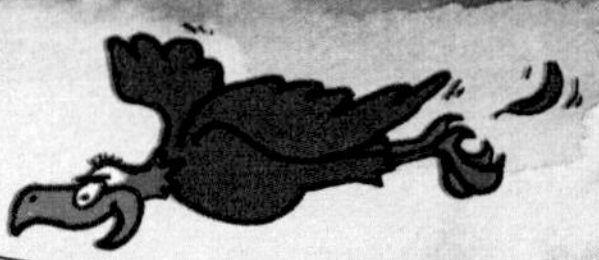

The whole story of the two kingdoms is a sad story, a story of the people turning their back on God and doing things that God had forbidden. It is a story of wars and sin and evil.

At Mount Sinai God had told the Israelites that they would live in the land as long as they obeyed God's commandments. But if they disobeyed God, the land would be conquered by their enemies and they themselves would be taken from the land. And that's what happened many years later.

First we'll see what happened to the northern kingdom, Israel, until it came to an end about 200 years later, and then we'll look at the story of the southern kingdom, Judah, which lasted for a little more than 300 years.

🐸 *1 Kings 11:41-12:33*

What king of Israel had the shortest reign? See 1 Kings 16:15.

Shechem

Woah—watch out! Don't get so upset, Chip. I didn't mean to make you feel bad.

Good—maybe with Jay in control we won't have so many mess-ups!

What's going on? What's wrong with Chip?

Come on, Brad. Chip's just pouting. He'll be OK.

Israel (The Northern Kingdom)

1 Kings

Jerusalem and the temple were in the southern kingdom. When the ten tribes decided to form their own kingdom, they cut themselves off from the temple where they were supposed to go to worship God.

Jeroboam, the first king of the northern kingdom, was worried that his people might still want to go down to Jerusalem to worship in the temple, so he immediately began to build altars in the northern kingdom, not for God, but for idols. He had a golden calf made for each altar, so that his people could worship at home – he didn't care that they would worship idols instead of God.

🐸 *1 Kings 12:25-33*

Where's Chip?

Oh, he'll be back.

Let's see if we can fly through this program.

OK. I'll punch "fly."

In Bible times, the best way to guarantee peace between two kingdoms was for one king to marry the other king's daughter or for a son of one king to marry a daughter of the other king.

We're Flies!

This bronze calf is an idol from the time of the northern kingdom. He's kind of cute, but why would anyone want to worship him?

I don't need them.

BLITZ!

What happened?!

Tracy must have messed up the program when she kept changing our clothes. Now even the computer is confused!

Great job, girls. Now what do we do?

n the first sixty years after King Solomon died, seven kings ruled over the northern kingdom. Two of them were assassinated and one, Zimri, had been king for only seven days when he killed himself by setting the palace on fire.

The seventh king, Omri, built the city of Samaria and made it the capital of the northern kingdom.

Ahab was the eighth king. He was more evil than any of the seven kings before him. He completely ignored God's commandments and married a foreign princess called Jezebel, who was even more wicked than Ahab himself. 🐸 *1 Kings 16:29-33*

Jezebel talked Ahab into making Baal, the god of the Canaanites, the official god of the northern kingdom.

The Canaanites believed that Baal was a cruel god who required human sacrifice. Before the walls of a city were built, for example, a child was killed and placed in the foundation of the wall, and another child was killed and placed in the foundation of the gates.

But God sent a man to speak out against Ahab: Elijah the prophet. 🐸 **Adventure reading:**

• Naboth's vineyard: **1 Kings 21:1-29**

S.W.A.T. TEAM

Names for Israel

The country where the Israelites lived has had several names over the centuries, which can be confusing. The whole country was at first called *Canaan* or the *Promised Land*. After the Israelites conquered Canaan the whole country was called *Israel*.

But after King Solomon's death, the name *Israel* meant only the ten tribes in the north (the southern part was called *Judah*).

Other names for the whole country are the *Holy Land* and *Palestine*.

CHIP! Help!

Hurry! Hostile Israelite sighted at 12 o'clock!

Where's the letter B?

Ouch!

The Prophet Elijah

Elijah came to King Ahab and told him that it wouldn't rain for several years. And it didn't. People and animals went hungry because nothing could grow. But God took care of Elijah: Ravens came and brought Elijah food, and he drank from a stream that still had water in it.

When the stream ran dry, God sent Elijah to a widow who had no food except for a handful of flour and a bit of oil – but the oil and the flour lasted and lasted, as long as it was needed. *1 Kings 17:1-24*

After several years of drought, it was time for a showdown between God and Baal.

On top of Mount Carmel there were two altars: an ancient altar for the Lord, and an altar for Baal built by King Ahab. On one side stood 450 prophets of Baal, on the other side Elijah, all by himself.

Two bulls were brought, and Elijah said, "You call to your god, and I'll call to my God, and the one who answers by sending fire down from heaven, he is God!"

So the prophets of Baal took one of the bulls, cut it into pieces, and put the pieces on Baal's altar. They began to pray and call out, "O Baal, answer us!" This went on from morning till noon. Then Elijah began to make fun of the priests of Baal: "Shout louder! Maybe Baal is asleep or on a trip." The prophets of Baal yelled louder and began to cut themselves with swords and spears so that they were bloody – they thought that Baal liked the smell of blood.

What is a prophet?

A prophet is someone who is sent by God with a special message. God sent prophets to tell the kings of Judah and Israel and the people to turn back to God and to obey him again.

The prophets also told what would happen if the kings and the people didn't turn back to God; the prophets thus predicted the future.

But even when the prophets said that God's judgment was coming, they also told of God's love and how in the end God would bring his people back to himself.

The prophets often began their speeches with: "This is what the Lord says." We know this from the seventeen books in the Bible that were written by prophets.

Archaeologists digging in ancient Samaria have found Ahab's palace – an incredibly beautiful building with all sorts of ivory decorations.

You're better off without your friends, kid. They didn't appreciate you anyway. Here, have some chips. Did I ever tell you the one about…

Trying to swat us, eh? Well, take this!

Jay! What buttons did you push, anyway?

I don't know! But at least we're getting bigger!

Push the buttons!

What Bible story are we on now?

The story of Elijah and the prophets of Baal.

Nothing happened. Finally, Elijah got up and built an altar with twelve stones (one for each tribe) and dug a small ditch around it. He put the wood on the altar and cut up the other bull and put the pieces on the altar.

Then he poured twelve large jars of water over the altar. If you have ever tried to set wet wood on fire, you know that Elijah made it very difficult for God. Elijah prayed one simple prayer – no yelling or shouting or dancing – and God sent fire down from heaven that burned not only the bull and the wood, but even the stones and the soil under it.

The people were convinced, and they chased the prophets of Baal and killed them. But Queen Jezebel was furious and wanted to kill Elijah, who had to run for his life.
1 Kings 18:16-46

If only my typing teacher could see me now!

Even today calling a woman a "Jezebel" is a terrible insult.

Baal

The Canaanites believed that Baal was the most important god. He was the storm god who controlled the springs and the rain and the thunder and lightning. In pictures and statues of Baal he often has a thunderbolt in one hand and a club in the other.

He was a terrifying god, the Canaanites thought, who sometimes wanted human sacrifices. People thought that if they displeased Baal, he would keep it from raining.

So when God first kept it from raining and then sent fire down from heaven, he showed everybody that he was real and Baal a fake.

The Prophet Elisha

2 Kings

Just you try typing with a beak!

King Ahab was killed in a battle. And Queen Jezebel? Fourteen years and two kings later, she was looking out of a window when Jehu, the new king, came driving by. Two of her servants threw her out of the window, and the horses trampled her. When Jehu gave orders to bury Jezebel, his servants came back shaken: the wild dogs that roamed the streets had eaten Jezebel, and all that was left were her skull, her feet, and her hands.
2 Kings 9:30-37

God was so pleased with what Elijah had done for him that Elijah didn't die like other people. Instead, he was taken up to heaven in a whirlwind, in a chariot of fire drawn by horses of fire. We can only imagine what it must have looked like, but it must have been awesome.
2 Kings 2:1-18
Elijah's place was taken by another prophet: Elisha. One thing we know about Elisha is that he was bald (read 2 Kings 2:23-25).

We said Baal, not ball!

Maybe I should've been more patient with them. After all, they didn't know what they were getting into.

Elisha performed quite a few miracles. For example, one time some friends of Elisha were chopping wood and an iron axhead fell in the water. Tools were made by hand and very expensive. Elisha threw a piece of wood in the water and the axhead came floating up! *2 Kings 6:1-7*
Adventure readings:
• The never-empty jar of oil: **2 Kings 4:1-7**
• The dead boy who sneezed: **2 Kings 4:8-37**

Later, Elisha helped the king of Israel to defeat the army of the king of Aram. The Arameans tried to attack the northern kingdom many times, but each time Elisha would tell the king of Israel where the Arameans would attack next, so the king was always prepared.

The king of Aram finally figured out what Elisha was doing and wanted to kill him. When he heard that Elisha was in the city of Dothan, the Aramean army surrounded the city at night. But Elisha wasn't worried. He saw that the hills around the army of Aram were full of horses and chariots of fire.

Elijah was one of only two people who went to heaven without dying. Who was the other one? See Genesis 5:24.

I'm a ping pong ball! Just hit a key! Anything's better than this!

Then Elisha asked God to make the army of Aram blind, and he walked out to meet them. He told the Arameans that they were in the wrong place and offered to take them to the right place. So he took them right into Samaria, the capital of the northern kingdom.

When the Arameans realized where they were they thought that they would be killed for sure, but Elisha told the king to let them go – after they had been treated to a big feast. And the Arameans quit bothering Israel, at least for a while.
2 Kings 6:8-23

Many of the kings of Aram were named "Ben-Hadad." "Ben" means "Son of" and "Hadad" is the name of the Aramean god of thunder.

I'll do my best!

But there is more. Naaman, one of the generals of the Aramean army, had leprosy – a terrible disease that couldn't be cured. His wife had an Israelite servant girl, who told Naaman's wife that there was a prophet in Israel who might be able to help Naaman.

So Naaman went to see Elisha, who thought at first that this was only a trick to get him in trouble with the king of Aram. But God told Elisha to help the Aramean general.

Naaman didn't like at all what Elisha told him to do: He had to go wash himself seven times in the Jordan River! Naaman had expected something really fancy or difficult, but seven "ducks" in a muddy river – they had better rivers in Aram!

His servants said, "Please, do it," and grumbling Naaman washed himself seven times – and was healed. Naaman promised Elisha that he would never worship any god but the Lord. *2 Kings 5:1-27*

This foreigner turned to the Lord, but the kings of Israel did not. Jehu, the king who had Queen Jezebel thrown out of the window, did destroy the altars of Baal, but that was as far as he went. He didn't serve the Lord, although he was better than almost all the other kings of Israel.

One king after the other ignored God and disobeyed God's law. God sent several other prophets, for example, Amos and Hosea, who wrote books that we still have in our Bible.

But it didn't help. Toward the end, two kings in a row were killed because someone else wanted to be king. One was killed after being king for only six months. His murderer ruled a month before he in turn was killed.

Finally, there was no turning back. For two centuries the northern kingdom had been attacked by the small nations around them. But during those centuries a much larger nation, an empire, had been growing in the east: Assyria. This huge empire was threatening to conquer Israel.

People are afraid of the word "leprosy." That is why the disease today is called "Hansen's disease."

Assyrians

The Assyrians liked war. They went out each year to fight, not because they wanted or needed more land, but because they needed money and slaves to build their great cities – especially Nineveh, their capital.

They were a very cruel people. When we talk about taking a "head count" we mean counting people. In war, the Assyrians would do a literal head count: soldiers would bring the heads of the enemies they killed to be counted.

How humiliating!

Froggo! Jump, boy! Jump on a button! Come on, boy! You can do it!

I didn't hear the magic word!

Jonah

And just as God showed kindness to Naaman, the general from Aram, so God showed kindness to the Assyrians. He gave the Assyrians a chance to change their ways and to turn to God. He told a prophet named Jonah to go to Assyria and to tell the people in Nineveh, its largest city, that Nineveh would be destroyed in forty days.

Jonah had a big problem. He knew that God was merciful and that if the people of Nineveh repented (turned to God), God would not destroy the city. But if the city was not destroyed, the Assyrians would surely come and destroy Israel – all because Jonah had preached in Nineveh.

Jonah tried to solve his problem by running away. Instead of going east to Nineveh, he went west on a ship. But God sent a huge storm, and Jonah told the sailors to throw him overboard to save the ship.

Jonah thought he would die in the sea, but God still wanted Jonah to go to Nineveh, so he sent a big fish to save Jonah. The fish swallowed Jonah (who prayed a lot), and three days later the fish threw Jonah up on the beach.

So Jonah finally went to Nineveh and preached – and sure enough, the people repented and the city was spared. But Jonah was mad at God! 🐟 *Jonah 1-4 (the whole book!)*

Where are we? What are we? Phew! What's that smell?

I think I have tentacles!

Dear Lord, please take care of my friends. Help me to find them…

Q: Who is the greatest wrestler in the Bible?

A: Jonah – even the great fish couldn't keep him down!

What Jonah had been afraid of happened. Some years later the Assyrians came and conquered Israel. They took away the people of Israel and sent people from other countries to live in Israel.

That was the end of Israel and the end of the ten tribes of the northern kingdom. No one knows for sure what happened to them – they vanished without a trace among the people of Assyria.

Twenty kings had ruled over Israel since Solomon, and not a single one of them had followed the Lord. Now, 200 years after Solomon died, the northern kingdom was no more. *2 Kings 17:1-19*

I don't want to know. I want Chip!

Where's the control box? Punch Chip's name in!

Jonah lived during the time of Jeroboam II, when Israel (the northern kingdom) was at its peak.

We have no idea what kind of fish swallowed Jonah, but it could have been a whale shark. (If you want to read about whale sharks and Jonah, find a copy of the National Geographic of December 1992.)

Judah (The Southern Kingdom)

Now we go back to the southern kingdom of Judah. After King Solomon died, things went a little better in Judah than in the northern kingdom. Some of the kings of Judah did follow the Lord, but there were also many kings who turned their back on God and did bad things. So the whole story of the southern kingdom goes back and forth between times when the people worshiped God and times when they worshiped idols.

When the ten tribes started their own kingdom, there had been a lot of people who left the northern kingdom and came to Judah because they wanted to be where the temple was and to worship God. And even when things got really bad in Judah, there were always people who were faithful to God.

Of the first five kings of Judah, only two did what God wanted. The sixth king was Ahaziah. His mother was the daughter of Ahab, the worst of the bad kings of the northern kingdom. Ahaziah was almost as bad as his grandfather Ahab. He was killed by Jehu, the same man who had Ahaziah's grandmother, Jezebel, thrown out of a window.

When Ahaziah was killed, his mother, Athaliah, decided that she wanted to be queen. So she simply killed the whole royal family of Judah. At least, that is what she thought. She missed one, a one-year-old boy named Joash, who for six years was hidden in the temple by his aunt and uncle. God's temple was the one place they could be sure Athaliah would never come!

When Joash was seven years old, his uncle called together a group of armed men, who stood around Joash in the temple as he was crowned king. The people cheered – they hated Queen Athaliah – and when the queen heard the noise she went to the temple (probably for the first time in her life) and saw what was happening. That was the last thing she saw, because the armed men took her outside the temple and killed her.

2 Kings 11:1-21

What was the largest army ever assembled in the Bible? See 2 Chronicles 14:9.

Joash was a good king who did what God wanted – but only as long as his uncle was around to tell him what to do. After his uncle died, Joash began to worship idols, and in the end he was killed by his own leaders.

After Joash came three good kings, but then came Ahaz, a king who was so bad that he even sacrificed his own son to Moloch, one of the old gods of Canaan! God warned Ahaz. He sent prophets such as Micah and Isaiah, who warned what would happen if he didn't turn back to God. But Ahaz wouldn't listen. 🐸 *2 Kings 16:1-4*

Kings & Chronicles

The stories of both the northern and the southern kingdoms are told in the books of Kings (1 Kings and 2 Kings). The books of Chronicles tell only the story of David, Solomon, and the southern kingdom.

Chip! I can't believe it! You're an answer to prayer!

Hi, Chip. Heh heh. Just a little glitch in the system here. Think you could help us out?

We missed you, Chip!

Chip! Where've you been, little buddy?

The next king of Judah was perhaps the best king since David and Solomon. His name was Hezekiah, and he was a friend of the prophet Isaiah. Hezekiah cleaned out the temple and made sure that the people of Judah worshiped God again.

But now the Assyrians, after conquering the northern kingdom, thought that they might as well keep going and conquer Judah also. They threatened, but Hezekiah was able to buy them off by giving them money and gold.

Then, one day, God told Hezekiah that he would die soon. But Hezekiah didn't want to die; there was still so much to do for the Lord and for his people. So he prayed, and God sent Isaiah to tell Hezekiah that God would let him live for fifteen more years. And God gave Hezekiah a sign. Each day, as the sun moved through the sky, Hezekiah could see the shadow of the building move slowly up the steps. But this day the shadow moved back down ten steps! *2 Kings 20:1-11*

The Assyrians came back. The army of Sennacherib, the Assyrian king, was camped all around the city of Jerusalem, and Sennacherib told the people in the city that they couldn't win and that their God couldn't save them. How wrong he was! In the night, the angel of the Lord killed 185,000 soldiers, and the Assyrians had to go back home in embarrassment.
2 Kings 18:17-37; 19:14-20, 32-37

112

Before Sennacherib attacked Jerusalem, Hezekiah cut a quarter-mile long tunnel through solid rock so the city would have water during a siege. That tunnel still exists.

Isaiah

The prophet Isaiah wrote a long book. The first part of the book of Isaiah (chapters 1-39) is full of gloom and doom.

Even though Isaiah's friend King Hezekiah was a good king who wanted to obey God, Isaiah knew that the people and the kings who came after Hezekiah would again become disobedient. Isaiah warned what would happen: the southern kingdom would be destroyed.

But the second part of the book of Isaiah (chapters 40-66) talks about the time after God has punished his people. The second part is full of hope and the promises of God's faithfulness.

Most important of all, Isaiah talks about God's Servant, the Lord Jesus, who will come and suffer and die for his people.

Isaiah 52:13-53:12

Adventure readings:

• God calls Isaiah, who is scared: **Isaiah 6:1-8**
• Isaiah sees the coming of John the Baptist: **Isaiah 40:1-11**
• Isaiah's funny description of idols: **Isaiah 44:12-20; especially verses 16-17**
• An invitation to you : **Isaiah 55:1-13**

LONG LIVE KING

SAUL
DAVID
SOLOMON
REHOBOAM
ABIJAH
ASA
JEHOSHAPHAT
JEHORAM
AHAZIAH
ATHALIAH
JOASH
AMAZIAH
AZARIAH
JOTHAM
AHAZ
HEZEKIAH

This is embarrassing. Now I see why the guys were so mad at us for dressing them up.

Yeah, I did get pretty carried away. We'd better apologize.

Hang on, you guys. It'll just take a minute to fix this. Besides, one chip around here is enough.

Jeremiah

If all the kings who came after Hezekiah had been like him and had obeyed God, the kingdom of Judah would have lasted. But of the seven kings who came after Hezekiah, only one really wanted to follow the Lord. His name was Josiah.

Josiah, who became king when he was only eight years old, did everything he could to bring his people back to God. And God sent a prophet, Jeremiah, to help him.

Josiah repaired the temple, and as the workmen were going through the building they found a book (it was actually a scroll) with the Law of Moses. No one had read God's Law for many, many years, so when the book was found Josiah called everybody together at the temple and read the whole book aloud. And the people agreed that they wanted to serve the Lord!

2 Kings 22:1-11; 23:1-3

But once again, things turned bad. The four kings who came after King Josiah didn't want anything to do with God. And Jeremiah got himself into trouble by warning that God would send a foreign army to destroy Jerusalem if the people didn't straighten out. The people didn't want to hear any bad news. They would rather listen to the false prophets who kept telling the people until the very end that everything would be fine, that God would never allow his temple to be destroyed. How wrong they were!

Those Judeans are lunch meat!

One of the last kings of Judah took the messages Jeremiah had written, cut them into pieces, and threw them into a fire (Jeremiah 36:1-7, 16-28). Jeremiah wrote them out again.

The Babylonians are coming!

Mommy, what's a "Bab bologna in"?

Babylonians? What Babylonians? I don't see any Babylonians!

Perhaps you are seeing things, sir?

I don't know, dear. I think that's something the prophets put in their sandwiches.

114

Jeremiah is one of the few prophets who not only wrote long sermons but also wrote about himself. When the Babylonians surrounded Jerusalem, the people kept saying, "God will deliver us because we are his people," and Jeremiah kept saying, "No, you haven't been listening to what God has being saying. God will not deliver you this time, because you have kept disobeying him!"

That is why the people (and especially the king) thought that Jeremiah was a traitor to his own people and threw him in prison.

Jeremiah didn't like what he had to tell the people. In fact, he cried a lot about what would happen. That is why Jeremiah is often called the Weeping Prophet.

Adventure readings:

• God calls Jeremiah who says, "But I'm only a kid!": **Jeremiah 1:4-19**
• Jeremiah is arrested: **Jeremiah 26:1-24**
• King Jehoiakim burns the books Jeremiah has written: **Jeremiah 36:1-32**
• Jeremiah is thrown in prison: **Jeremiah 37:1-21**
• Jeremiah is thrown into a mud hole to starve: **Jeremiah 38:1-13**
• Jerusalem is destroyed and the people are taken to Babylon: **Jeremiah 52:1-16**

In ancient times, the pages of a book were glued or sewn together to form a scroll — a long strip that was rolled up on both ends. This is a scroll of the Torah, the first five books of the Bible.

Babylonians, schmabylonians. I don't see any Babylonians!

Look! Babylonian spies!

Where? Where?

Hey, Chip, I'm sorry for all the mean things I said. You're really doing a great job.

Thanks, Trace. Sorry about all the program glitches.

That's OK, Chip. We're having fun. Really!

Like I was tellin' ya, Jerry, ol' bullfrog buddy, first those kids turned into flies, and then they were birds, and then…

Jerusalem is Destroyed

2 Kings

The Assyrians, who had conquered the northern kingdom, Israel, and who had taken the Israelites to Assyria, were a great and powerful nation for about 300 years. But another empire became even more powerful: Babylonia.

The Babylonians conquered Assyria and completely destroyed Nineveh, the great city where 120,000 people lived. They destroyed it so completely that for about 2,500 years nobody knew where it had been – until it was discovered again in the nineteenth century.

And now the Babylonians were about to conquer the southern kingdom, Judah. At first Nebuchadnezzar, the king of Babylon, came and took only a small group of people from Jerusalem to Babylon as hostages to make sure that the people of Judah wouldn't make trouble.
2 Kings 24:8-17

But about ten years later the last king of Judah tried to rebel against Babylon, so Nebuchadnezzar came back, killed the king, and completely destroyed Jerusalem and the temple. The southern kingdom was no more.
2 Kings 24:20b-25:12

Jeremiah didn't go to Babylon. He stayed in Jerusalem and wrote a very sad song about the fall of Jerusalem, which we still have in our Bible. It is called Lamentations. (Jeremiah later went to Egypt, where he died.)

Take off your blindfold, Nincompoop.

How deserted lies the city, once so full of people! See, O Lord, how distressed I am! I am in torment within.

Babylonians? What Babylonians? I don't see any Babylonians!

In 1903, archaeologists found tablets that gave Nebuchadnezzar's version of how King Jehoiachin was taken to Babylon. It is very similar to the version found in the Bible.

116

Lamentations

A lamentation is a very sad poem or song. Jeremiah, with tears in his eyes, wrote five poems about the things he saw when the Babylonians destroyed Jerusalem.

He saw children starving to death, young people and old people lying dead in the streets, fires burning everywhere (and no fire department to put them out). These things were happening to the people of Judah because of their sins.

But even when things couldn't get any worse, Jeremiah still trusted God. Have you ever sung the song "Great Is Thy Faithfulness"? Those words come from the book of Lamentations (3:23). Jeremiah was still able to tell the people that God loved them, that God would forgive them, and that God would keep his promise to bring his people back to Jerusalem.

Men? Have you something to say? Hmm?

Oh, oh, no sir, captain, I mean, um, general, um...

Psst. Great disguises, Chip. What's next?

According to his records, Nebuchadnezzar gave Jehoiachin and his family and servants lodging in his own palace.

It looks like the Babylonian soldiers are attacking a city by throwing bowling balls and pins over the wall, but these battles were actually very nasty.

In Babylon

Most of the people who were taken from Judah were given a place to live somewhere in the large country of Babylonia, along the Euphrates River. They now wished that they had listened to Jeremiah instead of to the false prophets!

But Jeremiah hadn't only been a "weeping prophet" who brought bad news. God had also given him a message of hope.

After the first people had been taken from Judah to Babylonia, Jeremiah had predicted that Nebuchadnezzar would be back and that almost all the people of Judah would be taken to Babylonia.

But it would not be forever! They would return after seventy years. That meant, of course, that almost all of the people who were taken to Babylonia would die there – but their children would return, and God would prove that he is faithful.

Here it is – Babylonia – home of one of the Seven Wonders of the World. For only a small additional fee, you can see the spectacular, the marvelous, the one-and-only Hanging Gardens of Babylon! Yes, that's right, for only $9.99 plus shipping and handling…BLAH BLAH BLAH

Why does Max keep popping up?

Can't you find some way to get rid of him?

I'll bring up the paint program. Maybe I can erase his character.

Moan. While you're at it, erase the camel too!

MAX'S BABYLONIAN CAMEL TOURS

The Oldest City in the World?

Babylon, the capital of Babylonia, may be the oldest city in the world. It was founded by Nimrod (Genesis 10:10), and it was the place where the Tower of Babel was built (Genesis 11:1-9). Babylon was located in what is now Iraq.

After the Babylonians conquered the Assyrians, King Nebuchadnezzar decided to make the city more beautiful than ever. And he did a great job of it! When he was done, the city was somewhere between 3 $\frac{1}{2}$ and 6 square miles in size – an awesome city for that time.

There were temples, palaces, and a gigantic "ziggurat" – which is not some kind of rodent but a square hill made of bricks, with a temple on top.

In Babylon you could also find one of the Seven Wonders of the ancient world: the Hanging Gardens of Babylon. (The pyramids of Egypt were another one of the seven wonders.) The gardens didn't really hang – they were planted on five terraces, each fifty feet tall.

But the Babylonian Empire didn't last very long – less than a hundred years. Then the Medes and Persians conquered Babylonia, and the Persian Empire took its place.

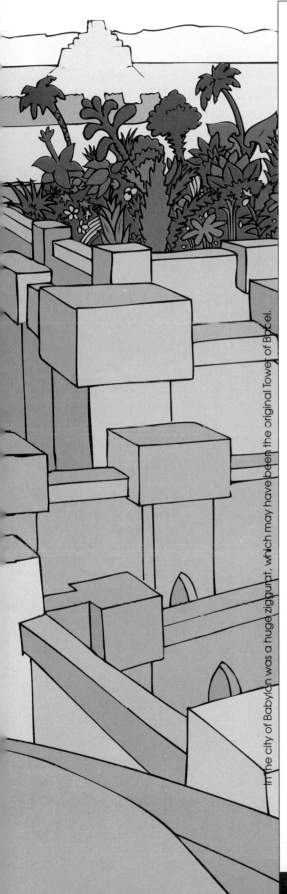

In the city of Babylon was a huge ziggurat, which may have been the original Tower of Babel.

This is a reconstruction of Babylon's main gate, the Ishtar Gate. The original gate was twice as large – wide enough for eight very fat camels (or two semis) to go through side by side.

Daniel

One of the hostages Nebuchadnezzar took back with him the first time he came to Jerusalem was Daniel, who was perhaps ten or twelve years old when he went to live at the court in Babylon.

The hostages had a problem. The Law of Moses said that the Israelites shouldn't eat certain foods, for example, pork. Daniel and his friends refused to eat anything the Law said they should not eat. And God made them healthier than any of the other boys who ate everything they were served. 🐸 *Daniel 1:1-21*

One night Nebuchadnezzar had a dream that really bothered him. He wanted to know what it meant, so his wise men said, "Tell us your dream and we'll tell you what it means." But the king said, "No way. You tell me what I dreamed last night. If you can tell me that, I'll know that you also know what it means."

Of course, the wise men couldn't do it, so the king was ready to kill all his wise men when Daniel heard what was happening. Daniel went to the king and God showed him what Nebuchadnezzar had seen in his dream: A huge, awesome statue with a head of gold, chest and arms of silver, belly and thighs of bronze, legs of iron, and feet of iron and clay. Then a huge rock came rolling down and smashed the statue – and the rock became a mountain that filled the whole earth.
🐸 *Daniel 2:1-19*

Daniel explained to the king that he was the head of gold, but that after him other kingdoms would come, not as strong and great as Nebuchadnezzar's, and that finally God would set up his own kingdom that would destroy all the others and fill the whole earth!
🐸 *Daniel 2:36-49*

The archaeologist Leonard Woolley found that the layout of the temple ruins of Nebuchadnezzar fit the Bible story with striking accuracy.

This is a 3,700-year-old Amorite school. Students sat on these backless stone benches and wrote by pressing styluses into soft clay tablets. When a student finished a lesson, he would "erase" his tablet by squishing it! (Girls couldn't go to school – I'm glad I didn't live back then.)

We're losing our color!

Hey! What's going on?

120

You'd think that Nebuchadnezzar would now realize that the God of Daniel was the true God. But no, he had a statue made, ninety feet tall, and he wanted everybody to worship the statue. Anybody who did not obey would be thrown into a blazing, red-hot furnace.

Daniel's three friends – Shadrach, Meshach, and Abednego – refused, and they were thrown into the oven, which had been made seven times hotter than usual. The oven was so hot that it killed the soldiers who threw Daniel's friends in it.

But the king had a surprise coming. When Nebuchadnezzar's servants looked inside, they saw Daniel's friends, not burnt to a crisp, but walking around in the oven, along with a fourth man (who was really an angel of the Lord). And after they came out of the oven, Nebuchadnezzar gave Daniel's friends a promotion and made a law that nobody could say anything against the God of the Israelites. *Daniel 3:1-30*

Look, Max got into the paint program!

He's taking big bytes out of our holographic program!

Hurry, Chip! Stop him!

Nebuchadnezzar restored Abraham's hometown of Ur in about 605-562 B.C.

An Ugly Statue Of Nebuchadnezzar

But Nebuchadnezzar just couldn't get it through his head that God is really in charge. He became very proud of Babylon, the great city he had built, and one day God had enough of his bragging. Nebuchadnezzar lost his sanity, and he became like a cow, grazing and eating grass for seven years. At last, when the king finally admitted that God was in charge, his sanity returned and he became king again. *Daniel 4:28-37*

After Nebuchadnezzar died, his dream of the great statue began to come true. Belshazzar became king, and Daniel, who was by now an old man, was still at the court. One night, during a huge feast, a hand appeared, writing on the wall of the room where the feast was held. Daniel explained what it meant: The great kingdom of Babylon was about to be conquered by the Medes and Persians and would no longer exist. And that's what happened. Nebuchadnezzar's great kingdom ended, and Darius the Mede became king. *Daniel 5:1-31*

A person who thinks he is an animal and lives out in the open fields suffers from "boanthropy."

Where are we?

Shudder. I think we're with Daniel in the lions' den.

Hi, kiddies! Are we having fun yet? Tell ya what. Let's make a deal. A hundred bucks, you can have your color back. Whaddaya say?

D arius, the new king, made Daniel one of the three most important people in the kingdom, and later the most important one – after the king, of course. The rest of Darius's officials were very jealous of Daniel.

They knew that Daniel served the Lord, and so they had King Darius make a new law that said that for a whole month people could not pray to any god – only to King Darius. The officials knew that Daniel would disobey the law, and sure enough, they saw Daniel praying to God as always.

They went to the king, who, much as he wanted to save Daniel, had no choice but to throw Daniel in the pit full of lions (the "lions' den"). But the lions didn't touch Daniel!

The king went to the pit early in the morning and found Daniel alive and well. So the king pulled Daniel out and had all the officials who had set the trap for Daniel thrown in the pit with their families – and the lions killed them before they even reached the floor of the pit.

Daniel stayed at the court of King Darius and also served under the next king, King Cyrus the Persian, who would later let the people of Judah go back home. *Daniel 6:1-28*

The Greek historian Xenophon also recorded the story of the handwriting on the wall.

Ezekiel

Jeremiah hadn't been the only prophet in Judah before the Babylonians came and destroyed Jerusalem. Another prophet was Ezekiel, who had been taken to Babylonia with the first group of people.

When Ezekiel heard that the temple had been destroyed, exactly as he had predicted, God told him to let the people know that they would one day go back to Jerusalem to rebuild the temple.

The prophet Ezekiel is best known for the strange and wonderful things he saw. For example, he had a vision of wheels within wheels that makes you almost dizzy when you read it, and he had a great vision of how God's people would come back to life – the vision of the dry bones.

Ezekiel also had a vision of a new temple, and he describes it, complete with exact measurements. Although the temple in Jerusalem was rebuilt seventy years after Nebuchadnezzar destroyed Solomon's temple, Ezekiel's temple is yet to be built.

Adventure Readings:
- The strange vision of wheels and creatures: **Ezekiel 1:1-28**
- The dry bones that come to life: **Ezekiel 37:1-14**

Ezekiel did some strange things. For example, he lay on his left side out in public for 390 days (more than a year!), and then he lay on his right side for 40 days (Ezekiel 4:1-8).

While he was living in Babylon, Ezekiel had a vision of God. This excited the Jews, because they thought God lived only in Jerusalem.

Back in Jerusalem

God kept his promise. Seventy years after the first Jews were taken away, King Cyrus of Persia, who now ruled over what had been the Babylonian Empire, said that the Jews could go home. Many of the Jews didn't want to leave Babylonia, where they had built homes and were comfortable, but 42,000 people went back.

🐸 *2 Chronicles 36:22-23* 🐸 *Ezra 1:1-4*

They thought it would be easy to move back home, but it wasn't. During the seventy years they had been away in Babylonia, other people had moved in and taken over the land, and they weren't too thrilled that the Jews were coming back. They made life very difficult for the returning Jews.

Although the people who came back started rebuilding the temple, they didn't get any further than the foundation. They simply lost interest and stopped. Jerusalem was a city without walls and a city without a temple. 🐸 *Ezra 3:7-4:5*

Two prophets, Haggai and Zechariah, kept telling the people not to quit, to finish the temple and to trust God, but the people were in no hurry, and it took twenty years before the temple was finally finished – seventy years after Solomon's temple was destroyed. The new temple wasn't nearly as beautiful as Solomon's temple, but the important thing was that the Jews could once again worship God in his own house in Jerusalem. 🐸 *Ezra 5:1-2; 6:1-12*

This five-mile long series of mounds is all that remains of what was once the largest, most elaborate city in the world: the great city of Babylon (see pages 118-19).

What happened? Did we commit a capital offense?

Chip – did you have to say "concrete" just before we blitzed?

Don't be afraid Froggo! Just hit the blitz button!

Guards! Arrest Haman!

Esther 8:9 is the longest verse in the Bible – with 71 words in the NIV.

Esther

While this was happening in Judah, there were still many Jews in Babylonia (which was now part of the Persian Empire). The book of Esther tells how God protected and saved even the Jews who didn't want to go back home – and yet God is never mentioned in the book of Esther.

King Xerxes of Persia (who became king after Darius, the king who had Daniel thrown into the lions' den) married Esther, a beautiful Jewish woman who had been adopted by her cousin Mordecai, a high official in King Xerxes' government.

But there was also Haman, another official in King Xerxes' government, even more important than Mordecai. Haman wanted people to bow to him when he came by – and everybody did, except Mordecai.

This made Haman furious. Haman knew that Mordecai was a Jew, so he decided that the best way to get rid of him was to get permission from the king to kill all the Jews in the whole Persian Empire.

But Mordecai found out what Haman was planning and asked Esther to help. After Esther told the king of Haman's plot, the king ordered Haman to be hanged on the gallows he had built for Mordecai.

But there was a bit of a problem. The king's permission to kill the Jews could not be changed (a law of the Medes and Persians was a law that couldn't be changed or canceled). So the king gave official permission to the Jews to defend themselves, and the Jews in Persia survived an attack that would have wiped them out.

🐸 Esther 2:1-11,17-23 🐸 Esther 3
🐸 Esther 4:1-5:8 🐸 Esther 6:1-14
🐸 Esther 7 🐸 Esther 8

Way to go, Esther!

Wow. That was a close call.

I'm sorry, King. I didn't mean it – really!

Hey, man! Leave her alone!

Help!

Each year on the feast of Purim, the Jews tell the story of Esther. Whenever Haman's name is mentioned, everyone boos loudly!

127

Q: Which Old Testament prophets were blind?

A: Hosea, Joel, Amos, Jonah, Nahum, and Habbakuk – none of them have I's.

The temple was finished, but all was not well. The Jews in Jerusalem did not follow God with all their heart, so God sent another prophet, Malachi (who wrote the last book in the Old Testament) to get the people to turn back to God. But it wasn't enough.

Sixty years after the temple was completed, a man named Ezra, who was a teacher of the Law of Moses, went from Persia to Jerusalem. (They hurried as fast as they could, but the trip still took five months.) Ezra preached in Jerusalem, especially against all the Jews who had married non-Jewish wives. (Remember King Solomon? That was where his problems began.)

Ezra preached, and the Jews listened. They agreed to send away all non-Jewish wives. The worship in the temple was restored, and things looked good – except that Jerusalem was still (eighty years after the first Jews came back) a city without walls, so that any enemy could easily overrun the city.

🐸 *Ezra 7:8-10; 10:1-4*

God now sent Nehemiah, who was a high official at the court of the Persian king Artaxerxes. The king gave Nehemiah permission to go to Jerusalem to rebuild the city walls. It was a good thing that Nehemiah had an official letter from the king because some of the people around Jerusalem didn't want the walls to be rebuilt. They were apparently afraid that the Jews would again become powerful.

🐸 *Nehemiah 2:1-10; 4:1-23*

Nehemiah did two things: He prayed to God for help, and he set guards around the city to keep the enemies from tearing the walls down again. Six months later the wall was finished, and Ezra read God's law to all the people.

🐸 *Nehemiah 6:15-19; 8:1-18*

Mediterranean Sea

Sea of Galilee

Zerubbabel

Ezra

Nehemiah

JERUSALEM

Dead Sea

Arabian Desert

The longest prayer in the Bible is the one recorded in Nehemiah 9:5-38.

Let's Live It

When we pray for God to help us, God doesn't expect us to sit back and do nothing. Nehemiah prayed, and then set guards and worked as hard as he could. If, for example, you have a test, ask for God's help and study as hard as you can.

Oomph!
Hey, watch your
elbow!

Elbow?!
Hey, we've been
de-columnized!

Why is it so
dark?

I think it's because
we've run out of stories from the
Old Testament.

But aren't
there more stories
after Esther?

Nope. That's the
last story. The rest of the Old
Testament is poetry and prophecies written
by people we have already met — like David,
Solomon, and Isaiah.

So the New
Testament is next, right? Let's go!
I want to see Jesus!

The story of the Old Testament ends with Nehemiah (Esther actually lived before Nehemiah). But when you look at the list of the books of the Old Testament in the front of your Bible, you'll see that Nehemiah is only halfway through the Old Testament.

That is because only the first seventeen books of the Old Testament tell the story of God and his people. The rest of the books of the Old Testament were written during the events that are described in the first seventeen books (the historical books).

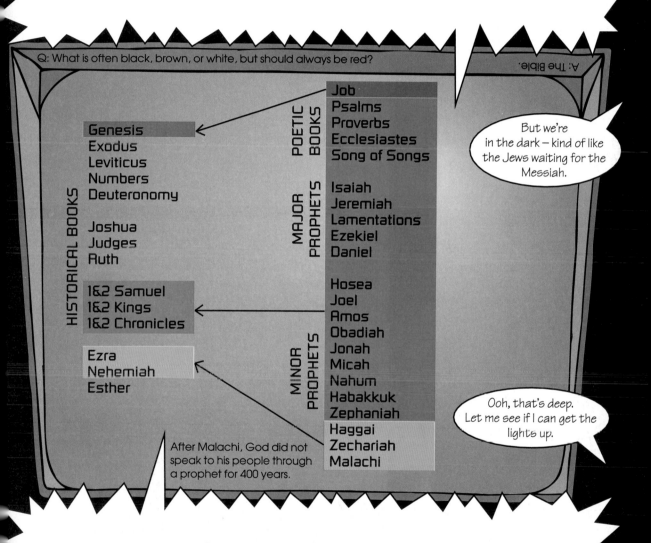

The rest of the books of the Old Testament are divided into three groups:
- the **poetic books** (Job, Psalms, Proverbs, Ecclesiastes, Song of Songs)
- the **major prophets** (Isaiah, Jeremiah, Lamentations, Ezekiel, Daniel)
- the **minor prophets** (Hosea, Joel, Amos, Obadiah, Jonah, Micah, Nahum, Habakkuk, Zephaniah, Haggai, Zechariah, Malachi)

The arrows show where the rest of the Old Testament books fit into the historical books.

Between the Testaments

At the end of the Old Testament,
- the Persians are in charge
- there is only a small temple in Jerusalem
- there is no king over Judah
- everybody speaks Hebrew

At the beginning of the New Testament,
- the Romans are in charge
- there is a beautiful temple in Jerusalem
- King Herod rules over Judah (which is now called Judea)
- there are several religious groups, especially the Pharisees and Sadducees
- most people speak Greek
- the land is divided into two parts: Galilee in the north and Judea in the south (with the Samaritans in between)

After King Cyrus of Persia let the Jews go back to Jerusalem, the Persians were in charge for another hundred years. Then they themselves were conquered by the famous Alexander the Great, who conquered more countries than anyone had ever done before him.

Alexander the Great came from Macedonia near Greece, and he decided that everybody in his huge empire (which included Palestine) should act like Greeks and speak Greek. And it worked. When the New Testament was written 300 years later, it was written in Greek, because that is what everybody could read.

But Alexander's empire fell apart, and about a hundred years later Palestine was ruled by the Syrians (which is not the same as the Assyrians). And that's when the fun began.

One of the Syrian kings, with the fancy name Antiochus IV Epiphanes, decided that everybody should worship the Greek god Zeus. So he put a big statue of Zeus in the temple in Jerusalem, and he sacrificed a pig on the altar — which was terrible, since God had told the Jews that pigs are unclean animals and unclean animals should never be sacrificed to God.

This was too much for the Jews. Five brothers, known as the Maccabees, decided to fight Antiochus. To everybody's surprise they captured Jerusalem, threw the statue of Zeus out of the temple, and rebuilt the altar of the Lord in the temple. (The Jews today still celebrate this event every December with the Feast of Hanukkah.)

Finally, almost 400 years after the Babylonians killed the last king of Judah and took the Jews to Babylon, Palestine became a free country again, this time ruled by the high priest instead of a king.

But that lasted only about seventy-five years, until two brothers both wanted to be high priest. They both asked for help from Rome (which had grown into the largest empire the world had ever seen – even larger than Alexander the Great's empire).

It turned out to be a really dumb idea, because the Romans did help, but they figured that as long as they were in Palestine, they might as well make Palestine a part of the Roman Empire!

So now the Romans were in charge, even though they allowed Herod to be king – as long as he did what the Romans wanted.

How do you say "Do you have any Alka-Seltzer" in Hebrew?

So that was 400 years, huh?

H-Hey, C-Chip, s-stand s-still a m-minute, w-would y-you? Y-you're m-making m-me d-dizzy.

Help! I'm falling and I can't get up!

Hoo-wee! Was that a ride or was that a **ride!** Fantastic!

135

"Maccabee" is a Hebrew word meaning "hammer." The Maccabees really hammered the Syrian rulers until they won the war.

There are quite a few things in the New Testament that didn't exist yet in Old Testament times.

Synagogues

Before the Jews were taken to Babylonia they worshiped God in one place: the temple in Jerusalem. But the temple was destroyed by the Babylonians, so the Jews in Babylonia invented the synagogue, which is somewhat like our church.

Every town had its own synagogue where people got together to read from the Jewish Bible (our Old Testament) and to pray.

After the Jews returned from Babylon, they rebuilt the temple, but they also kept the synagogues. They visited the temple only once or twice per year, but they went to the synagogue every week, on the Sabbath.

Hmm, I never knew text boxes could be so comfy. Zzzzz.

Yawn. That last blitz really wore me out!

Wake me up when we get to the good part.

Pharisees and Sadducees

When Alexander the Great decided that he wanted everybody in his empire to speak Greek and to act like Greeks, many Jews didn't like it. They knew that God wanted them to be Jews, not Greeks, and that many things the Greeks did were against God's Law.

The Jews who didn't want to have anything to do with Greek ideas and who wanted to stick with God's Law came to be known as the Pharisees.

The Sadducees, on the other hand, were a group of important Jews who didn't think that Greek things were all that bad, and they didn't worry about keeping God's Law too exactly.

This synagogue in Galilee is over 1,700 years old – and it looks like it!

Sanhedrin

The Sanhedrin was something like a combination of our Congress and Supreme Court. The Sanhedrin was in charge of everyday life in Palestine, including religious matters.

The seventy-one members of the Sanhedrin were Pharisees and Sadducees. The high priest was the president of the Sanhedrin. (It was the Sanhedrin that condemned Jesus to death.)

Time for an intertestamental snooze. Zzzzz.

Wait a minute, Jay! I'll have us snoozing in style...

So many Jews lost their ability to speak Hebrew that eventually a group of scholars translated the Old Testament into Greek; this version is called the Septuagint.

Samaritans

The Samaritans lived in Samaria, between Judea in the south and Galilee in the north. They were a mixture of the Israelites that had been left behind when the Assyrians took away the ten tribes of the northern kingdom and people who had come from other countries.

The Samaritans worshiped God, but they believed that the place to worship was not Jerusalem but Mount Gerizim. The Jews thoroughly disliked the Samaritans, and the Samaritans didn't like the Jews a whole lot either.

I loaded my flight simulator program. Now we can just fly through the rest! Fasten your seatbelts, everyone!

Another ruin! (I like to imagine what things must have looked like before they became ruins.) This is what is left of the original walls of Samaria, built 900 years before Christ.

Will this add points to my frequent flyer program?

ZZZZ ZZZZ

ZZZ ZZZZ

I love flying first class...

Oh, oh! Got caught in first class!

Herod was so suspicious and jealous of other people that he killed even his own wife and his two sons, because he thought they wanted him dead.

King Herod the Great and the Temple

King Herod the Great liked building things. He built palaces for himself in Jericho and near the Dead Sea at Masada. He also built the Herodion, a round fortress that was made by hollowing out the top of a mountain. He even built a whole new city, Caesarea, named after the emperor, Caesar.

Herod was not a very religious man – in fact, he wasn't even a Jew but an Idumean. He tried to make the Jews like him by making the temple in Jerusalem as beautiful as he could. (It didn't work – the Jews never liked him anyway.)

By the time Jesus was born, people had been working on the temple for twenty years, but all that had been finished was the temple building itself. There were still courtyards and walls and covered walkways to be built – it would take another fifty years before everything was finished, many, many years after King Herod died.

The sad thing is that the completed temple would stand for only six years before it was completely destroyed by the Romans in A.D. 70.

Part of the walls of Herod's temple are still standing. To get an idea how big it was, look at the picture of what is known as the Wailing Wall, where to this day Jews come and pray. The Wailing Wall is only a small section of the bottom part of the walls of the temple court.

At the edge of the temple the Romans built the Antonia Fortress with towers that overlooked the temple area so that they could keep an eye on things.

Back in the Garden of Eden, after the Fall, God promised Adam and Eve that one of their descendants would defeat Satan and make things right again between God and his creation. ✦ *Genesis 3:15*

Ever since then, God's people had been waiting for this deliverer, called the Messiah. (*Messiah* is a Hebrew word that means "Anointed One"; if you don't remember what *anointed* means, look at page 75.)

At the time Jesus was born, the Jews were anxiously waiting for the Messiah to come. The problem was that the Jews expected a Messiah who would deliver God's people from the Romans with a huge army and who would once again make Israel a powerful nation.

But when Jesus, the Messiah, came he was very different from what everybody expected, and most of the people didn't like it at all.

The Greek word for *Messiah* is *Christ.* So when Peter tells Jesus, "You are the Christ," what he really says is, "Yes, you are the Messiah, the One we have all been waiting for!"
🐸 *Matthew 16:13-16*

Now **that's** what I call "falling asleep"!

Too bad the parachutes were terminated too-oo-oo-oo!

I say the Messiah will come as a king.

I say the Messiah will come as a wise, scholarly king.

I say the Messiah will come as a wise, scholarly, **conquering** king!

What does "gospel" mean?

Gospel means "good news." The gospel is the good news that God sent his son Jesus to take away our sins by dying on the cross.

But gospel can also mean the story of Jesus' birth, life, death, and resurrection. There are four gospels in the Bible, written by Matthew, Mark, Luke, and John.

> Is this a nightmare? Or reality? Or a hologram? Or a movie? HELP! I need to know what's REAL!

Charles Dickens, the author of *A Christmas Carol*, said, "The New Testament is the very best book that ever was or ever will be known in the world."

> Head towards Bethlehem!...What am I saying? FEET towards Bethlehem!

> Boy, even the flight movies are holographic. I actually feel like I'm falling.

Why are there four gospels?

Even all four gospels put together tell only a small part of the story of Jesus (read John 21:25). Each of the four gospels is written for different people.

Matthew's gospel is written for Jews and shows that Jesus is the Messiah, since he fulfilled the things that were foretold about the Messiah. Mark's gospel is for anyone who doesn't know about Jesus. It's full of action and often uses words like "immediately" and "as soon as." Luke's gospel is written for people who are not Jews. It talks about how much Jesus cares for poor people and for people nobody else likes. John's gospel is very different. It uses simple words but is very profound. John shows that Jesus is the Son of God.

The gospels show that "Jesus was the kindest, tenderest, gentlest, most patient, most understanding man that ever lived. He loved people. He hated to see people in trouble. He loved to forgive. He loved to help. He did marvelous miracles to feed hungry people. The many tired, confused, and hurting people who came to him found healing and relief. That is the kind of man Jesus was. That is the kind of person God is. And that is what the Bible (and especially the New Testament) is all about" (H.H.Halley).

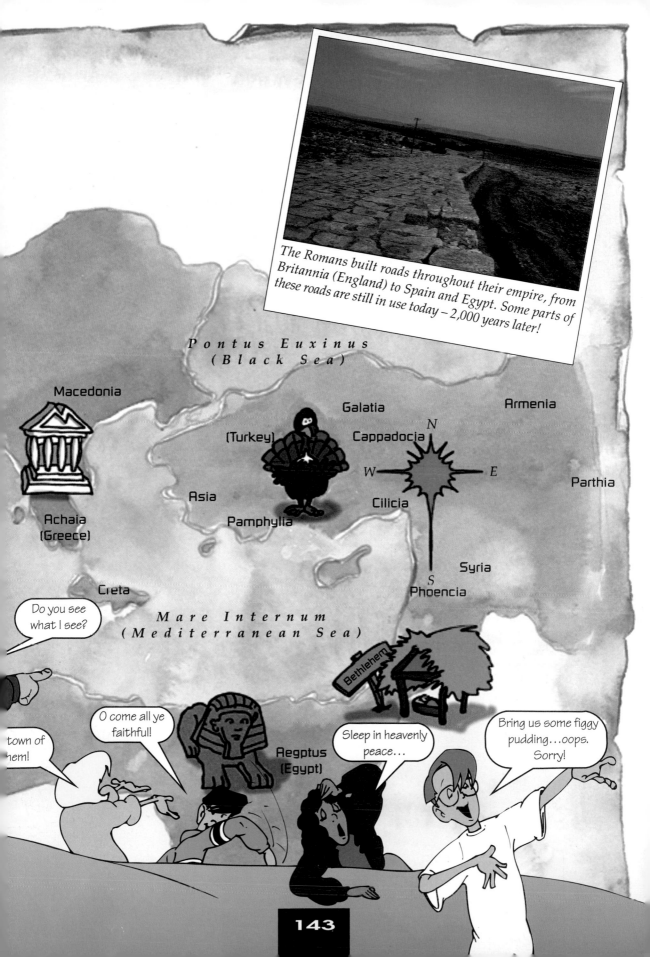

The Romans built roads throughout their empire, from Britannia (England) to Spain and Egypt. Some parts of these roads are still in use today – 2,000 years later!

Pontus Euxinus
(Black Sea)

Macedonia

Galatia

Armenia

(Turkey)

Cappadocia

N

Asia

W   E

Parthia

Cilicia

Achaia
(Greece)

Pamphylia

Syria

S

Creta

Phoencia

Mare Internum
(Mediterranean Sea)

Bethlehem

Do you see
what I see?

O come all ye
faithful!

Sleep in heavenly
peace...

Bring us some figgy
pudding...oops.
Sorry!

town of
hem!

Aegptus
(Egypt)

Birth of John & Jesus

The Gospels

Zechariah was a priest. He was all alone in the temple when suddenly an angel stood beside him, and Zechariah was scared – who wouldn't be? The angel told him that he and his wife, Elizabeth, would have a son – who would be a prophet. There had not been a prophet in Israel for 400 years, but now God would speak to his people again!

Zechariah had a hard time believing the angel because he and his wife were very old. So the angel said, "You won't be able to speak until your son is born." And sure enough, when Zechariah stepped outside to bless the people he could only wave his hands – he couldn't say a word! *Luke 1:5-25*

When his son was born, Zechariah wrote that his son's name would be John (as the angel had told him) and suddenly Zechariah could speak again. The first thing he did was to sing a beautiful song: John would be a prophet of the Most High who would tell the people how their sins could be forgiven and how they could be saved! *Luke 1:57-80*

Bethlehem as it looks today. Back when Jesus was born, only a few hundred people and lots of sheep lived here.

Frankincense and myrrh, two gifts the Wise Men brought, were perfumes made from tree sap. They had to be imported from Arabia and only VERY rich people could afford them.

Joy to the world! The Lord is come!

The same angel who appeared to Zechariah had a message for a relative of Zechariah's wife – a young woman named Mary in the small town of Nazareth. The angel told Mary that she would also have a child. Mary was confused – "But I'm not even married!" she said. The angel told her that her child would be a miracle.

His name would be Jesus (which means "The Lord Saves"). He would be the Son of God, and God would give him the throne of David. He would be a king! David's kingdom had fallen apart, but the kingdom of Jesus would never end. And Mary, who would be the mother of Jesus, was willing to obey God. *Luke 1:26-38*

Just before Jesus was born, the Roman emperor decided that he wanted to know how many people lived in the Roman Empire.

Everybody had to go to the town where their family originally came from. Mary and her husband, Joseph, whom she had just married, had to go south to Bethlehem because their family – the family of King David – came from there.

They had to travel almost 100 miles, a trip that took them more than a week. When they came to Bethlehem, all the other people whose families originally came from Bethlehem had already arrived, and Joseph and Mary couldn't find a place to stay. They finally found room in a stable (probably in a cave), and there Mary had her baby, Jesus, God's Son, who was born to be a king! *Luke 2:1-7*

Dating events B.C. (Before Christ) and A.D. (Anno Domini, "in the year of our Lord") was begun by Dionysius Exiguus around A.D. 525.

In Bible times newborn babies were wrapped in long bandages from the navel to the feet because it was believed that leg movements would harm a baby's soft bones. They were the "swaddling clothes."

The first people to hear about the birth of Jesus the Messiah were shepherds (shepherds were not respected in Palestine!). The shepherds told everybody who wanted to hear – and even those who didn't – about what they had seen and heard. 🐸 *Luke 2:8-20*

God also used the stars to tell of Jesus' birth. Three scholars from the east (perhaps from Persia) , who studied the stars, one night saw a star that told them that a king of the Jews had been born.

They traveled to Jerusalem to ask King Herod about this new king. Herod asked the scribes and the Pharisees, who studied the Old Testament. They told Herod that the prophets had said that the Messiah would be born in Bethlehem.

So to Bethlehem the wise men from the east went. They found Jesus and worshiped him and gave him very expensive gifts. 🐸 *Matthew 2:1-12*

King Herod also went to Bethlehem – not to worship Jesus but to kill him. If God hadn't warned Mary and Joseph to leave Bethlehem and go to Egypt for a while, he would have succeeded, because he ordered his soldiers to kill all children in Bethlehem who were under two years old. This was the same man who rebuilt the temple of the Lord. 🐸 *Matthew 2:13-18*

When Mary, Joseph, and Jesus came back from Egypt, they returned to Nazareth, where Jesus grew up. 🐸 *Matthew 2:19-23*

🐸 **Adventure reading:**

• Jesus is presented in the temple: **Luke 2:22-42**

We know very little about how Jesus grew up. He had brothers and sisters and was for many years a carpenter, like Joseph. There is only one story in the Bible about Jesus as a boy.

When Jesus was twelve he went for the first time to the temple in Jerusalem, like every grown-up Jew was supposed to do. (A Jewish boy was considered grown-up at age twelve.) From Nazareth to Jerusalem is almost as far as from Nazareth to Bethlehem – about ninety miles, or more than a week's travel.

On the way home, Joseph and Mary were walking along with a large group of people who had also been to Jerusalem, when they suddenly realized that they hadn't seen Jesus for quite a while. They asked around, but Jesus was nowhere to be found.

They went back to Jerusalem, worried that something terrible had happened to Jesus. But when they got there, they found Jesus sitting in the temple, talking with the teachers of the law (some of whom were Pharisees). He listened to them and asked them questions, and they were all amazed at how much Jesus knew about the Word of God and how much he understood.

When Mary and Joseph asked Jesus why he had stayed behind, Jesus said, "Didn't you know that I had to be in my Father's house?"
Luke 2:41-52

Sea of Galilee

Nazareth

Jordan River

When Jesus was twelve...

N
W   E
S

Mediterranean Sea

Jerusalem

Bethlehem

Dead Sea

Hebron

To Egypt

Jesus had brothers and sisters; at least two of his brothers later became his followers and wrote the books of James and Jude in the Bible.

John the Baptist
The Gospels

Repent, for the kingdom of heaven is near!

By the time Jesus was baptized, his earthly father, Joseph, had probably already died; that is why we never read about him again in the Gospels.

After-school snack, anyone? Just watch out for the legs – they tend to get stuck between your teeth.

Jesus had been a carpenter for quite a few years when he heard that his cousin John, the son of Zechariah, had begun to preach near the Jordan, east of Jerusalem. John lived simply: He ate wild honey and grasshoppers (which are actually a good source of protein), and he wore a simple coat of camel's hair.

His message was simple too. John told people to repent (turn back to God) so that their sins would be forgiven. And when people said, "Yes, I want to obey God," John baptized them in the Jordan River. That is why he was called John the Baptist.

It was surprising how many people came from Jerusalem to listen to John. But when the Pharisees came to see him, he called them a bunch of snakes who were trying to sneak away from God's anger. He told them that being a Jew wasn't enough – not even being a Pharisee was enough! They had to prove that they had repented by doing good deeds. *Matthew 3:1-10*

John knew that the people were wondering deep down if he was the Messiah. But he kept telling them, "I'm not the Messiah – but he's coming after me, and he will baptize you with the Holy Spirit instead of with water." *Matthew 3:11-12*

LOCUST

B ut then, one day, John looked at the people listening to him, and he saw Jesus standing in the crowd. He pointed to Jesus and said, "Look, the Lamb of God, who takes away the sin of the world! He is the one I was talking about."

And then Jesus asked John to baptize him (even though he did not need to repent!), and when John did, the sky opened and the Spirit of God came down like a dove and rested on Jesus. And a voice came from heaven that said: "This is my Son; I am very pleased with him."

🐸 *John 1:29-31* 🐸 *Matthew 3:13-17*

🐸 **Adventure reading:**
• John the Baptist in prison: **Luke 3:19-20**
   Matthew 14:1-13

This is the Jordan River where John baptized Jesus.

Did you see the ancestors of the Pharisees on page 43?

No, I can't see Jesus. Can you see Jesus?

I can't see anything!

Did you give John permission to baptize people?

I didn't give him permission. Did **you** give him permission?

I didn't give him permission. Maybe **he** gave him permission. Did **you** give him permission?

I can't see Jesus. Can you see Jesus?

No, I can't see Jesus. Can you see Jesus?

Would you guys please stop that?

Jesus' Ministry Begins

The Gospels

In the Garden of Eden, Satan had talked Eve into disobeying God. And now Satan tried to do the same with Jesus. Satan knew that if he could get Jesus to disobey God, God's plan to save the world through Jesus would fail. Satan tempted Jesus, just as he tempts us to disobey God.

Jesus was hungry, and Satan said, "If you are the Messiah, you can make bread out of these rocks!" He tried to tell Jesus that Jesus could have (and deserved to have) whatever he wanted!

Then he took Jesus to the top of the temple wall and said, "If you really are the Messiah, you can jump down, and God will send his angels to save you." He tried to convince Jesus that he could do whatever he wanted, and nothing bad would happen!

Finally, Satan took Jesus to a high mountain to show him all the powerful kingdoms of the world and said, "I'll give you all these kingdoms – all you have to do is worship me." Satan tried to get Jesus to choose the power of this world (which lasts only until somebody else comes along who is stronger) instead of the power of love and truth and honesty, which lasts forever! *Matthew 4:1-11*

Not a McDonald's in sight…How did people ever survive in this place?

Maybe we'll find Jesus if we follow this map.

I don't know. It's awfully hard to navigate through a wilderness. Remember the camel treks across the desert? And that long walk to Bethlehem?

Don't remind me.

Now Jesus also began to preach. Like John the Baptist, Jesus preached about the coming kingdom of God, when the whole world will obey God. He told people to get ready for that kingdom by turning to God, by repenting.

The people expected the kingdom of God to be a kingdom like the Roman Empire, except even stronger, with soldiers and wealth and power. And the Messiah would be the king.

But Jesus told the people that the kingdom of God is an "upside-down" kind of kingdom – not at all like the Roman Empire, but a kingdom where God rules in the hearts of his people and where people who seem to be the least important are really the most important.
Luke 9:46-48 *Luke 17:20-21* *John 18:36-37*

And Jesus showed the people what God is like by healing people, and by caring for the poor and for people without power, and by not being too busy to listen to and talk with kids.

Jesus also wanted people to know that what he was telling them was not only for the Jews – it's for everybody, even the Samaritans and the Gentiles (non-Jews).

Not yet.

Do you see any sign of Jesus?

The Disciples

The Gospels

When Jesus began to preach, he chose twelve men who would travel with him and whom he would teach. They were to be Jesus' disciples. (Jewish teachers, called rabbis, didn't choose their own disciples – the students chose the rabbi they wanted to learn from.)

🐸 *Mark 1:14-20* 🐸 *Mark 3:13-19*

If you had met these twelve men, you wouldn't have thought that they were anything special. They weren't terribly important, they hadn't gone to school for many years, and they didn't know a lot of important people. But to Jesus they were very special.

Jesus showed that God doesn't care how important or how smart or how popular people are. He uses people who know they're not very important or bright or popular.

Jesus chose twelve disciples to help him. Later, after Jesus returned to heaven, the disciples would become the apostles.

The list of disciples is kind of confusing, because there are two Simons, two disciples called James, and two disciples called Judas (or Jude).

Peter, also known as Simon and Simon Peter, the leader of the disciples; Peter loved Jesus, but he could be hot-headed and didn't always think before he acted. (Read, for example, John 18:10-11, where Peter did something that was neither smart nor helpful.)

Andrew, the brother of Simon Peter.

Matthew, also known as Levi, who wrote the first gospel; he was a tax collector before he met Jesus (read Matthew 9:9-13).

Disciples? Humph! They're barely out of Sunday school!

5 more disciples

Simon, also known as Simon the Zealot, which may mean that before he met Jesus he belonged to a terrorist group known as the "Zealots."

There are more Jews living in the United States than in the country of Israel today.

John, the disciple who was Jesus' special friend. He wrote one of the four gospels, and John and Peter were the leaders of the early church.

James, the brother of John.

Philip, who was from the same small town as Peter and Andrew – they grew up together.

Bartholomew, probably the same as Nathanael, Philip's friend who wasn't so sure about Jesus at first (read John 1:43-51).

Thomas, also known as Didymus, is often called "Doubting Thomas" because after the Resurrection he found it hard to believe that Jesus was really alive (read John 20:24-29).

James, about whom we know nothing except that his father's name was Alphaeus. This is not the James who wrote the book of James in the Bible – that was Jesus' brother James (who wasn't one of the twelve disciples).

Judas, the son of James.

Judas Iscariot, who betrayed Jesus and later killed himself.

Like the disciples, modern fishermen on the Sea of Galilee fish at night, shining lights to attract the fish and capturing them in nets.

The Parables of Jesus

The Gospels

Jesus told a lot of stories to make people understand what he was teaching. These stories are called "parables."

For example, Jesus spent time with people everybody looked down on. He talked with Samaritans, with tax collectors (whom everybody hated), with all kinds of people nobody wanted to be friends with.

The Jews thought that God didn't want them to talk with people like that. So Jesus told a story to try to make the Jews understand that God wants to save the people who are lost.

He said, "If a shepherd has a hundred sheep and one of his sheep walks off and gets lost, the shepherd will leave the ninety-nine sheep and do his very best to find the one lost sheep." God is like that shepherd. He always tries to find people who have run away from him and he tries to bring them back to safety. And that is why Jesus talked with sinners: He did his very best to find people who were far away from God and to bring them back to God.

He said, "Look, healthy people don't need a doctor, but people who are sick do." 🐸 *Luke 15:1-7* 🐸 *Luke 5:27-31*

The Parable of the Prodigal Son shows that God is like the best father you can imagine: When we go away from him and do things that are stupid or bad, he waits for us to come back, and he gives us a big hug (even when we smell like pigs) and celebrates because he is happy we're back.
🐸 *Luke 15:11-32*

The Parable of the Sower and the Seed is explained by the Lord Jesus himself. 🐸 *Matthew 13:1-23*

Hey, gang, it's a pair of bulls. Parables, pair o' bulls. Get it?

Is there a law against bad bull puns?

I don't know. But get me a bull point pen and I'll write one.

The Parable of the Good Samaritan shows that when God says, "Love your neighbor like you love yourself," you shouldn't make things complicated by trying to figure out who your neighbor is. Your neighbor is anybody who needs your help – anybody you meet, whether rich or poor, nice or nasty. 🐸 *Luke 10:25-37*

The Parable of the Weeds shows that you can't always clearly tell who belongs to God's kingdom and who doesn't. Sometimes people who seem to be very good Christians are really not, and people who seem to be far from God may be very close to him. 🐸 *Matthew 13:24-30*

Olive oil was used to soften skin, and as a remedy for cuts, wounds, and burns. The Good Samaritan poured oil into the wounds of the injured man.

The Parable of the House Built on the Rock shows that no matter how beautiful your life may look from the outside, if you don't trust God it will fall apart. 🐸 *Matthew 7:24-27*

Is Jesus the Messiah?

The Gospels

It took the twelve disciples a long time to understand who Jesus really was! Like everybody else, they expected a Messiah who would kick the Romans out and make Israel a powerful kingdom again – at least as powerful as it had been under King David.

But Jesus didn't try to make friends with the powerful people. He wasn't interested in politics and he didn't try to build an army. Instead, he made friends with people nobody thought were important or even likable.

Could this really be the Messiah, the one they all had been waiting for? Jesus talked about God's kingdom, but it was a very different kingdom than they expected. The kingdom Jesus talked about was not a kingdom with an army and strong cities. Jesus preached about loving and caring for others. His kingdom was not a kingdom of this world at all.

If you had been alive when Jesus walked around Palestine, preaching about this kingdom, would you have believed him? It's like expecting to get a present when your parents come back from a trip. But instead, when they come home, they give you a big hug and tell you how much they missed you and how much they love you. It would probably take a while before you understood that being loved and cared for is a whole lot more important than getting a video game.

That's what the disciples must have felt like. They expected God to show the Romans a thing or two, but instead God showed the people that he loved them. It took a while, but finally the disciples began to understand.

This is Jerusalem today. The Dome of the Rock, a mosque, stands where the temple once stood. The Mount of Olives is behind it.

Who do you think Jesus is?

156

One day Jesus asked the disciples, "Who do people say that I am?" And they told him that most people thought that he was one of the prophets who had come back to life, perhaps Elijah. But when Jesus asked them, "Who do you think I am?" Peter said, "You are the Messiah, the Son of the Living God!" (*Christ* is the Greek word for "Messiah.") 🔱 *Matthew 16:13-20*

But that didn't mean that the disciples now understood everything Jesus was trying to teach them. For example, one time Jesus found them arguing about which of them was most important. Jesus didn't get mad at them, but he said, "If you want to be really important in God's eyes, you must be willing to be the least important in the eyes of people!"
🔱 *Mark 9:33-37*

Archaeologists have found small baked clay figures that may have been dolls. They have also found rattles, whistles, model animals, and chariots that were probably children's toys.

The disciples still didn't get it. One day there were a lot of people around Jesus, and some kids wanted to see Jesus. The disciples thought that Jesus was too busy to talk with kids, and they tried to chase them away. But when Jesus saw what the disciples were doing, he said, "Let those kids come over here! God's kingdom isn't just for adults – it's for kids as well!" What's more, Jesus said, You adults must become like these kids who want to come to me and talk with me and listen to me. 🔱 *Mark 10:13-16*

The Miracles of Jesus

The Gospels

Jesus did many miracles – things people thought just don't happen, like dead people coming back to life again.

Jesus didn't do miracles to show off or to impress people. He did miracles for the same reason he told parables: to help us understand what God is like.

Jesus went around healing people. He made blind people see and deaf people hear, and people who couldn't walk he made to walk again. And he made people free who were possessed by evil spirits.

Jesus did miracles to show that God cares – not only about big things but also about little things. The first miracle Jesus did was to make wine out of water because he wanted to keep his mother's friends from being embarrassed. 🐸 *John 2:1-11*

One day, Jesus was walking along the road when he saw people going to a funeral. A young man had died, and his mother was left all alone. Jesus took the cold hand of the young man (Jews weren't supposed to touch a dead body!) and he came back to life. 🐸 *Luke 7:11-16*

Jesus became a celebrity. If he were alive today, people would want to interview him on TV and on talk shows.

Jesus once fed five thousand people with the lunch a boy had brought. Jesus began breaking the bread and the fishes into pieces, and he just kept on doing it until everybody had had enough to eat. There was more food left over than he started with! 🐸 *Mark 6:32-44*

Jesus made a man see who had never been able to see in his whole life. Jesus spit on the ground and made some mud that he put on the man's eyes, and when the man washed his eyes, he could see. 🐸 *John 9:1-34*

Normally peaceful, the Sea of Galilee sometimes has waves up to six feet high when winds swoop down from the hills.

Another time Jesus was talking with people when a leader of the synagogue came to him and told Jesus that his daughter was so sick that she would probably die. Before Jesus could get to the house, someone came and said, "It's too late, she's already dead." But Jesus went to the house anyway and told the mourners to go outside. He took the girl by the hand and said, "Get up, little girl!" And she jumped up and walked.
Mark 5:21-43

Once the disciples were in a boat on the Sea of Galilee in a bad storm. If you have ever been in a small boat in a storm you know how frightening it is. But then Jesus came walking across the waves. (Seeing Jesus walking on the water may have scared them even more than the storm did!) Jesus climbed in the boat, and they safely reached the shore. *Matthew 14:22-33*

Maybe these printouts will give us a clue about where Jesus is. What are you reading, Tracy?

About the blind man. Can you imagine what it would be like to see for the first time in your life?

I can't figure out why we can't get close to Jesus.

Yeah — all we see is what he's done. It's like we keep arriving a couple minutes too late.

Hmm... Loaves and fishes. Fishwiches!

Like everybody else, Jesus had to pay a tax for the temple. So Jesus told Peter to go fishing, and in the mouth of the first fish he caught would be a coin that would pay both Jesus' and Peter's temple tax. *Matthew 17:24-27* esus didn't just talk about God, he showed people what God was like.

He healed people and made people alive again to show that God cares for us and that he is more powerful than sickness and even death.

He stilled the storm to show us that God is stronger than the most powerful forces of nature.

He fed five thousand people because he wanted to show that God can give us the things we need every day.

That is what God is like!

Of course, not everybody who saw the miracles believed in Jesus. Some of the Pharisees who saw Jesus cast evil spirits out of people said, "This is all a trick! The master of the evil spirits, Satan himself, helps him do that."

Other people didn't really want to believe in Jesus, but they liked to watch him do miracles – they thought it was a great show.

But there were also people who saw what Jesus did and heard what Jesus said who believed that he was really the Son of God, the Messiah.

Ten lepers were healed, but only one said "Thank you"!
Luke 17:11-19

Some of the famous Jewish rabbis claimed to be able to do miracles, but none of them ever claimed to be able to raise dead people back to life.

Jesus told Simon Peter, who hadn't caught a single fish the whole night, to try one more time – and Peter caught so many fish that the nets almost broke.
Luke 5:1-11

A lame man who couldn't make it to the pool was healed and walked away carrying his mattress. *John 5:1-15*

Jesus healed two men possessed by evil spirits – which ended up in a bunch of pigs.
Matthew 8:28-34

Jesus brought three people back to life: a little girl, a boy, and an older man.

Jesus healed a man's deformed hand – but the Pharisees complained because he did it on the Sabbath, the day of rest!
Matthew 12:9-14

I think I found Jesus! The control box says he's preaching the Sermon on the Mount right now. Let's go!

What Jesus Taught

The Gospels

For a while, Jesus was very popular. People came from all over to listen to him talk about the kingdom of God and tell the people how they should live.

Jesus wasn't a boring teacher. He told stories and parables to make people understand what he was saying. In the four gospels we find a lot of what Jesus taught.

The Sermon on the Mount is the longest sermon in the Gospels. It begins with nine sayings, each of which begins with "Blessed are . . ." (The Latin word for "blessed" is *beatus*, which is why these sayings are called the Beatitudes.)
🐸 *Matthew 5:1-12*

In the Sermon on the Mount, Jesus also taught his disciples how to pray. He told them not to show off when they pray and not to use a lot of fancy words. He taught them a wonderful, simple prayer, the Lord's Prayer (sometimes also called the "Our Father," because that is how it begins). 🐸 *Matthew 6:5-15*

At Sinai, God had given the Israelites laws. Of all those laws, which are the most important? Jesus said that two of the laws were more important than all the others. If people didn't keep those two laws it wouldn't do a lot of good to keep all the rest. The first is:

> You must love the Lord your God with all your heart, soul, and mind.

And the second one, which is just as important, is:

> You must love your neighbor the way you love yourself.

You cannot love God and not love your neighbor. Remember – your "neighbor" is anyone you meet.
🐸 *Mark 12:28-34*

The two laws that Jesus said are the most important are also found in the Old Testament. (See Deuteronomy 6:5 and Leviticus 19:18.)

Tradition says this is where Jesus preached the Sermon on the Mount.

🐸 **Adventure Readings:**
- Jesus is rejected in his hometown Nazareth: **Luke 4:13-30**
- Jesus teaches Nicodemus: **John 3:1-21**
- Jesus talks with a Samaritan woman: **John 4:4-42**
- Eating with sinners and tax collectors: **Matthew 9:9-13**
- Is Jesus really Christ (the Messiah)?: **Matthew 16:13-20**
- The Transfiguration: **Luke 9:28-36**
- Who is the greatest?: **Mark 9:33-37**
- Mary and Martha: **Luke 10:38-42**
- The little children and Jesus: **Mark 10:13-16**
- The rich young man: **Mark 10:17-22**
- Little Zacchaeus: **Luke 19:1-10**
- The greatest commandment: **Mark 12:28-34**
- The widow's offering: **Mark 12:41-44**

Quick, Brad, give me a boost! I think I can see him!

OK, but you boost me next.

The Pharisees

I didn't give them permission. Did **you** give them permission?

Did you give them permission to sit on your palm on the Sabbath?

One group of Pharisees was so strict they were nicknamed "Bleeding Pharisees." They were so determined never to sin that they walked around with their eyes closed!

The Jewish leaders – especially the Pharisees – couldn't stand Jesus. Which was strange, because if you met a Pharisee, you'd think he was wonderful. The Pharisees went to the synagogue (the Jewish church) every week, prayed more than anybody else, and knew the Jewish Bible (our Old Testament) from cover to cover.

They talked about God and they prayed to God and they were very careful to keep God's Law – so why did they hate Jesus, the Son of God?

The problem was that they loved the Law of God more than they loved God himself. And they didn't love people the way Jesus did – they just wanted to make sure that people kept God's laws.

The Pharisees were so worried that people might break the law that they made lots of new laws, just to make sure. For example, God told the Jews that they shouldn't work on the Sabbath. But the Pharisees made a long list of exactly what things the Jews could not do on the Sabbath (which left a very short list of what they could do).

The Pharisees wanted to impress people. They were always showing off how special they were, how well they obeyed the law, and how much they prayed – they would even pray right on the street corners! 🌿 *Luke 11:37-46*

Whoa! Give this guy some Certs!

Check out the size of that mug!

Chip! Try "palm trees," not just palm!

OK, here goes.

I didn't give them permission. **You** must have given them permission. After all, they're on **your** palm.

The Pharisees said that walking further than three quarters of a mile on the Sabbath was a sin.

The Pharisees hated Jesus because Jesus told them (and everybody else) that the Pharisees were not as wonderful as they thought they were.

Jesus once told a parable about a Pharisee and a tax collector. Everybody disliked tax collectors because they worked for the Roman government. The Romans would tell the tax collectors how much money they had to get from the people, and the tax collectors would then ask for even more and keep the difference for themselves, so that they got very rich.

The Pharisee in the parable was standing in the front of the synagogue, praying, "God, I thank you that I am not like this tax collector; I thank you that I am a good person."

The tax collector didn't pray that way at all. He said, "God, please have mercy on me because I am a sinner – I'm no good." And Jesus said that God heard the prayer of the tax collector, because he really prayed to God, but he didn't listen to the Pharisee, who only wanted to tell God that God should be impressed with him because he was such a terrific person. *Luke 18:9-14*

The Pharisees knew that if the people listened to Jesus they would no longer listen to the Pharisees, and the Pharisees would lose their power. Or the Romans might get upset and take away the power of the Jewish leaders.

So the Pharisees and the other leaders decided that it was about time they did something about Jesus!

Jesus and the Pharisees

The Gospels

The Pharisees wore little boxes on their foreheads and on their arms that contained verses from Exodus and Deuteronomy. (See Deuteronomy 6:4-8 for the reason why.)

It was the week before the Passover, the most important feast of the year, when the Jews remembered how, many centuries ago, God had delivered them from Egypt under Moses.

Jesus came into Jerusalem, riding on a donkey. The people went wild. They treated him like a king. They took off their coats and put them on the road; they cut branches off the palm trees along the road and put those down as well. (The palm branch was the symbol of royalty and of Jewish nationalism.) They shouted, "Hosanna to the Son of David," which means, "God bless the Son of David!" The whole city was excited – everybody except the Pharisees.

They saw what happened and thought for sure that Jesus would start some sort of rebellion that could only lead to trouble with the Romans.

And then, to make things worse, Jesus walked into the temple court and made a scene. In the temple court merchants changed money and sold animals for sacrifices so people could give their gifts to God. Jesus walked in and turned their tables

upside down, so that everything rolled over the floor. The temple was for worshiping God; it should be a house of prayer, not a place where people could make money.

🐸 *Matthew 21:1-16*

This was too much for the Jewish leaders. They came to Jesus and asked him, "Who has given you the right to do all of this?" They still didn't understand that it was God himself who had given Jesus authority and that they weren't fighting a carpenter from Nazareth but the Son of God.

Instead of answering their question, Jesus asked them, "Tell me first, was John the Baptist sent from God or not?" The Jewish leaders said to themselves, "If we say that John was sent by God, then Jesus will say, 'Why didn't you listen to him?' And if we say, 'He wasn't sent by God' then the people will come after us, because they believe that John was a prophet from God." So they chickened out and said, "We don't know." So Jesus said, "Then I won't answer your question either!"

🐸 *Matthew 21:23-27*

But they tried again to trick Jesus. They asked him, "Is it right to pay taxes to Caesar, the emperor of Rome?" This was a difficult question because if Jesus said no, the Jewish leaders could turn him over to the Romans for treason; but if he said yes, then the people would get mad at Jesus because they would think that he liked the Romans.

Jesus' answer surprised everybody. He said, "Why are you trying to trick me? Show me a coin." So one of the Jewish leaders handed him a coin. Jesus asked, "Whose picture and name are on this coin?" They said, "The picture and name of Caesar, the emperor."

Why was it important whose picture was on the coin? The Jews believed that it was wrong to put anybody's picture on anything, and Jewish coins from before the time of the Romans only had a palm branch on them. But now the Pharisees showed that when it came to money they were willing to ignore their own laws – they used money with a picture of Caesar on it!

So Jesus said, "Why don't you give back to Caesar what belongs to Caesar – but give to God what belongs to him!" The Jews were so embarrassed that all they could do was walk away.

Matthew 22:15-22

Among the taxes Jews had to pay were a land tax, poll tax, property tax, customs tax, and temple tax. Jerusalem residents also had to pay a house tax.

Judas was the treasurer of Jesus' group of disciples, but he also stole some of the money to spend on himself (John 12:1-6).

Every time they tried to get Jesus to say something that would get him in trouble, Jesus' answer would embarrass them. They were getting fed up, and at a meeting at the home of the high priest they decided that the best thing to do would be to kill Jesus. But they knew they had to do it quietly or else the people might start a riot.

Somehow Judas, one of the twelve disciples, heard what the Jewish leaders were planning. He went to them and said, "How much will you pay me if I tell you how you can catch Jesus quietly, without the whole city knowing what is going on?" They agreed on thirty silver coins (which, by the way, was the fine for accidentally killing someone else's slave in Old Testament times).

Matthew 26:1-5,14-16

Oops – wrong emperor! This coin shows Vespasian, who was emperor about thirty years after the Pharisees argued with Jesus. (But then, when you've seen one emperor you've seen them all.)

169

The Last Supper

It was the night before the Passover, the feast that celebrated God's delivering the Israelites from Egypt. On that night each Jewish family got together to eat the Passover dinner. Jesus and his disciples were eating the Passover meal in the house of a friend.

Because the roads and the unpaved streets of Jerusalem were very dusty, people washed their feet before they ate. Usually this was done by a servant, but this time Jesus took a towel and began washing the disciples' feet. They were embarrassed, but Jesus showed what he had been preaching about: If you really want to be a leader, you have to become a servant.
John 13:1-17

While they were eating, Jesus said, "One of you will betray me." He gave Judas one last chance to change his mind. But Judas' mind was made up. He left and went to the Jewish leaders (who should have been celebrating the Passover meal!). Judas told them that they could find Jesus in the Garden of Gethsemane, just outside of Jerusalem.
John 13:21-30

As they were eating, Jesus took a piece of bread, broke it, and said, "Take and eat;

One of the worst sins in Bible times was to betray a friend with whom you had just eaten a meal.

Leonardo da Vinci (1452-1519), The Last Supper, Santa Maria della Grazie, Milan this is my body." Then he took a cup of wine and said, "Drink of it, all of you. This is the new covenant [agreement or contract] in my blood, which is poured out for many for the forgiveness of sins." You have probably heard these words in church during what some people call the Lord's Supper and others call Communion. What did Jesus mean?

Matthew 26:26-29

In the Garden of Eden, God had said that the penalty for sin is death. And when God made a covenant with the people of Israel at Mount Sinai, God told the Israelites to bring sacrifices every day for their sins – an animal would die in their place on the altar.

The sacrifices were a sign that the people wanted to obey God; God then would forgive their sins.

But now God was about to make a new covenant, a new agreement, not just with the people of Israel, but with all people, no matter who they were or where and when they lived.

This new covenant doesn't ask for sacrifices every day. It needs only one sacrifice, provided by God himself: his own Son, Jesus. Jesus died once and for all in our place.

All we have to do is say, "Thank you!" to God for his sacrifice, and when we do something wrong, we can tell God and he has promised to forgive us! That is what Jesus meant when he told the disciples to eat the bread and drink from the cup.

Jesus is Betrayed

The Gospels

In the Garden of Gethsemane on the Mount of Olives, Jesus prayed to ask God if it might be possible for him to be spared the suffering and death he knew would come soon. But Jesus also said, "Not my will, but yours be done!" Jesus had to suffer alone – the disciples had fallen asleep! 🐸 *Luke 22:39-46*

Soon a large group of men came, armed with swords and clubs. Judas was with them. He walked up to Jesus and kissed him, so that the armed men would know who they should arrest. And then Jesus said the saddest words in the Bible: "Judas, do you betray me with a kiss?"

To the people who came to arrest him, Jesus said, "Why are you coming with swords and clubs to arrest me as if I were a criminal? Here I am." And the disciples? They ran away. 🐸 *Luke 22:47-53*

Wow! That Giotto guy lived over 700 years ago!

Isn't it cool? Back then most people couldn't read, so they would learn the story of Jesus by looking at paintings like this!

Yuck! – Peter's chopping off that guy's ear.

Giotto (1266-1337),
The Kiss of Judas,
Arena Chapel, Padua

According to Matthew, Judas merely hanged himself. But Luke's account of his death in Acts 1:18 is more descriptive – and quite disgusting!

Judas

Judas had been with Jesus for three years but had never really understood him. Judas thought that Jesus was the Messiah – but he thought that Jesus should do what everybody wanted the Messiah to do: get rid of the Romans and make Israel a country with a king again.

When he saw that Jesus didn't want to be king and would not get rid of the Romans, he lost interest. He didn't understand who Jesus really was, and he didn't want to understand. We don't know if he realized that the Pharisees wanted to kill Jesus.

The Pharisees gave Judas thirty silver coins to tell them where they could catch Jesus without too many people being around. But after Jesus died on the cross, Judas realized that he was guilty of Jesus' death and became so desperate that he killed himself. ❧ *Matthew 27:3-10*

These coins are exactly like the ones Judas got for betraying Jesus. Thirty pieces of silver were worth about five months' wages (or five years' wages when you work part-time at Burger King).

Jesus' Trial

The Gospels

Gustave Doré
(1832-1883)
The Mocking of Jesus

The mob that came to arrest Jesus took him to the home of Caiaphas, the high priest. The whole Supreme Court of the Jews, the Sanhedrin, was there – even though they were not supposed to meet at night.

But they had a problem. They had to come up with a reason to kill Jesus. There were quite a few people who accused Jesus of different things, but their stories didn't agree with each other. Finally, the high priest got frustrated and asked Jesus, "In the name of the living God, are you or are you not the Messiah, the Son of God?"

And Jesus said, "Yes, I am." Then the high priest tore his clothes and said, "He has spoken blasphemy" (which means, he has insulted God). "You have all heard it. What should we do?"

And the Supreme Court said, "Kill him! He deserves it!" They finally had the excuse they needed to put Jesus to death – even though Jesus had only said what was true. *Mark 14:53-65*

Just a few hours before Peter said that he didn't know Jesus, he had promised Jesus that he would never desert him (Mark 14:27-31).

W hile this was happening inside, something else went on outside, in the courtyard of the house of the high priest. Peter, Jesus' disciple, had come into the courtyard to be near Jesus. He was probably ashamed for running away when Jesus needed him.

But while he was sitting there by the fire, trying to keep warm, suddenly somebody asked Peter, "Aren't you one of Jesus' disciples?" Peter was afraid because he was trapped. And he said, "No!" But it happened two more times, and the third time Peter was so scared that he said, "Look, I don't even know this Jesus!"

And then a rooster crowed, and Peter remembered that at the Last Supper Jesus had said, "Peter, you're going to say that you don't know me three times before the rooster crows." Peter ran away, crying his eyes out.

Mark 14:66-72

He could have called an army of angels to wipe out all his enemies, but he didn't.

Yeah, he was a king who cared more for us than for power or money.

That's horrible. I can't stand to see Jesus mocked like that!

Wow! So that's what real strength is.

Jesus Before Pilate

The Gospels

The Sanhedrin had condemned Jesus to die, but now they had another problem – only the Romans were allowed to actually put him to death. So now the Jews had to convince the Romans that they should kill Jesus.

They took Jesus to Pontius Pilate, the Roman governor of Judea. They told Pilate that they wanted him to execute Jesus. Pilate, of course, asked, "Why?" and the Jews said, "Look, if he weren't a criminal we wouldn't bring him to you." So Pilate asked Jesus the same question the high priest had asked earlier: "Are you the King of the Jews, the Messiah?" And Jesus again said, "Yes."

Pilate didn't want to condemn Jesus to death, but he also didn't want to upset the Jews. So he thought he would be sneaky and give the Jews a choice between a real criminal called Barabbas and Jesus; he would let one go free. But the Jews didn't do what Pilate expected – they chose Barabbas! *John 18:29-38*

Pilate tried one last thing to keep from having to kill Jesus. He sent Jesus to King Herod. But Herod sent Jesus right back. He didn't see any reason to kill Jesus either.

Pilate still wanted to set Jesus free, but the Jews began to yell loudly that they would tell the emperor in Rome about this. Pilate became afraid that he might lose his job, so he finally gave in.

The Roman soldiers mocked Jesus; they pressed a crown made of branches with thorns down on his head and dressed him up like a king.
Luke 23:6-16

Pilate once made the Jews angry by taking money that was meant for the Temple and using it to build a twenty-five mile aqueduct to bring water into Jerusalem.

The only place anyone had ever seen Pontius Pilate's name was in the Bible – until a few years ago, when a stone was found in Caesarea with his name on it.

Victims of crucifixion died by suffocation when they no longer had the strength to breathe air into their lungs.

Rembrandt (1606-1669),
The Three Crosses,
Rijksprentenkabinet,
Amsterdam

Death by Crucifixion

One of the nastiest ways to kill someone is crucifixion: to tie or nail the person to a cross. Crucifixion is really a way to torture as well as to kill a person. Death comes very, very slowly – it can take two or three days for the person to die, and those days are agony.

Sometimes the Romans would attach a block to the cross on which the victim could partially sit and sometimes also a block on which the victim could stand. But this would only make things worse, because as long as the victim could support some of his weight, the blood could still circulate.

When the Romans wanted to make a crucified person die faster, they would break his legs with a club below the knees, so that he could no longer support himself. Soon his heart would simply stop beating.

The Romans crucified slaves and very bad criminals. A few years later, the Romans would crucify many of Jesus' followers, and many people believe that the apostle Peter was crucified upside-down.

The floor on which Jesus probably stood when he was on trial. Roman soldiers

scratched the game in the floor. The winner could do anything to a prisoner he wanted to. (It got so bad that soldiers were later forbidden to play it.)

The Crucifixion

The Gospels

They made Jesus carry his own cross to a hill outside the city wall: Golgotha (another name for Golgotha is Calvary). There they crucified him. Sometimes the Romans tied the victim to the cross, but often they actually put nails through his hands and feet – and that is what they did with Jesus.

There were three crosses on Golgotha. Jesus was in the middle, between two robbers. Pilate was still upset that the Jews had forced him to crucify Jesus, so he got even with the Jews by putting a sarcastic sign on Jesus' cross that said, "This is the King of the Jews." He wrote it in three languages, so that everybody would be able to read it. *Luke 23:26-27* *John 19:17-27*

Jesus' last words on the cross were, "It is finished!" He had come to save the world, and he had nearly completed his task. Satan used people to kill Jesus, but when Jesus died he won the battle between Satan and God! By dying, Jesus showed that God's love is greater than Satan's hate. *John 19:28-30*

The Roman soldiers were surprised that Jesus had died so quickly. One of them stabbed Jesus with a spear, and blood and water came out, which showed that Jesus was dead. *John 19:31-37*

Jesus' friends buried him in a grave – a small cave with a large round stone that could be rolled in front of the opening to close the cave.

The strange thing was that Jesus' enemies remembered something that his disciples had forgotten. They remembered that Jesus had said that he would rise again after three days. So the Jews asked the Romans to put soldiers in front of the tomb. They didn't really believe that Jesus would come back to life, but they thought that his disciples might try to steal the body so that they could tell everybody that Jesus had come back to life. *Matthew 27:57-66*

"Golgotha" is an Aramaic word, and "Calvary" is a Latin word; both mean "skull."

178

If you go to Jerusalem today, guides will show you two different caves, both empty, where Jesus is thought to have been buried.

A crown of thorns, much like the one Jesus was made to wear.

Michelangelo Caravaggio (1571-1610),
The Entombment,
Pinacoteca Vaticana, Rome

Jesus is dead.

They killed him.

He suffered so much...

All because we sinned.

He loved me enough to die for me...

The Resurrection
The Gospels

It was now Sunday morning. Jesus had been buried on Friday, and Jerusalem was quiet again. The soldiers at the tomb were looking forward to going home. But suddenly the earth shook, and the soldiers saw an angel come down and roll away the stone from Jesus' tomb. They were scared out of their wits and ran away as fast as they could!

When the Jewish leaders heard what had happened, they told the guards to tell everybody that they had fallen asleep and that the disciples had come and stolen the body. (Anybody could know that that wasn't true, because any Roman soldier who fell asleep while on duty would be killed immediately!)

The first people to come to Jesus' tomb on Sunday morning after the guards had run away were three women who were followers of Jesus. They came and saw that the heavy stone had been rolled away! When they walked in, they saw a young man (who really was an angel) sitting inside. He said, "Don't be scared! Jesus is risen! Tell Peter and the other disciples."

So they told Peter and John, who came running to the tomb and saw that Jesus was gone – that he was risen!

Matthew 28:1-16

Giotto (1266-1337), The Resurrection, Arena Chapel, Padua

A tomb with a stone that rolls in front of the opening to close it. The track slants downward, so it is much harder to open the tomb than to close it.

More than 500 people saw Jesus alive again after he had been crucified (1 Corinthians 15:6).

Jesus is Alive!

Jesus appeared to his disciples many times during the next few weeks. One time was especially important for Peter, who had denied three times that he knew Jesus.

The disciples were in a boat. Peter never could sit still for very long, so he had decided to go fishing. The disciples still didn't understand that this was not the end but the beginning. They didn't know that they would see the message of Jesus spread through the whole world.

They had been fishing all night and hadn't caught a thing. Then, when they came close to the shore, they saw a man sitting on the beach who told them to throw the net on the other side of the boat. They did, and the net was suddenly so full of fish that they couldn't haul it to the shore!

And then Peter said, "It's the Lord!" He jumped overboard and waded to shore. It was Jesus, who had breakfast all ready for them.

After breakfast Jesus asked Peter, "Peter, do you love me more than these other men do?" And Peter said, "Yes, Lord, you know that I love you." Then Jesus asked Peter the same question two more times, and the last time Peter said, "Lord, you know all things; you know that I love you!" Of course Jesus knew that Peter loved him. But Jesus wanted Peter to know that he really and truly loved Jesus, even though he had said, "I don't know him." And Jesus wanted Peter to know that he loved Peter and that he still wanted Peter to be his disciple. *John 21:1-25*

What are those gold things on their heads?

Ha! The soldiers slept right through the Resurrection!

Halos — that's how artists used to show that these were God's special people.

Women were not allowed to be witnesses in a Jewish trial, but God made them the first witnesses of the resurrected Jesus!

The Ascension

Acts

T he disciples could still hardly believe that Jesus was really alive. They saw Jesus many times during the forty days after the Resurrection, and Jesus taught them more about the kingdom of God.

But the disciples still didn't understand how different Jesus was from the Messiah the Jews were expecting. They still worried about the wrong things – they asked Jesus, "Are you going to make Israel a kingdom, a free country again?"

Jesus said, "That is the Father's business. But you will receive power when the Holy Spirit comes, power to tell others about me and about what God has done – not just here in Jerusalem but everywhere!"

A few days later, when Jesus and the disciples were standing on the Mount of Olives, Jesus went to heaven before their eyes. The disciples went back to Jerusalem, where they and the other followers of Jesus (about 120 people altogether) prayed and waited, as Jesus had told them to do.
🐸 *Acts 1:1-11*

Then suddenly early one morning, it sounded like a hurricane was blowing through the house. What looked like flames settled on the head of each of them. These were signs showing that the Holy Spirit had come, as Jesus had promised!

Jerusalem was full of people, Jews who had come from all over the world to celebrate the Feast of Pentecost. They went to see where the sound came from and found the house where Jesus' followers were, who looked excited and happy and were all talking.

Other people have been raised from the dead, but later on they died again. But not Jesus!

The amazing thing was that these uneducated Jews were praising God in languages they didn't know, so that all the foreign Jews could understand them.

Then Peter began to talk. "Some of you think we're drunk, but we're not – it's only nine in the morning! What you see here is what the prophet Joel said would happen. God has sent his Spirit to show that Jesus, whom you crucified a few weeks ago, is alive and is truly the Messiah, the one you have all been waiting for."

When Peter finished, someone asked, "What should we do?" And Peter said, "Turn away from the bad things you have done and believe in Jesus the Messiah. And to show that you believe in him, be baptized in his name. Your sins will be forgiven and you'll receive the Holy Spirit – which will show that you made the right decision!"

Three thousand people believed and were baptized. So on the first day, the church grew from a small group that could fit in a house to a crowd so large that the only place large enough for them to meet in was the temple court!
🐸 *Acts 2:1-24, 32-36, 41*

You mean he's already with us?

That's right! He's with us now, even if we don't see him! That's why the computer couldn't show him.

Do you really think that will work?

Jesus said, "I am with you always, to the very end of the age." Matthew 28:20.

I've got it! Use the computer's search command to find Jesus!

It's worth a try.

Since Judas had killed himself, the disciples picked someone else to fill his place and make the number of the disciples twelve again (Acts 1:12-26).

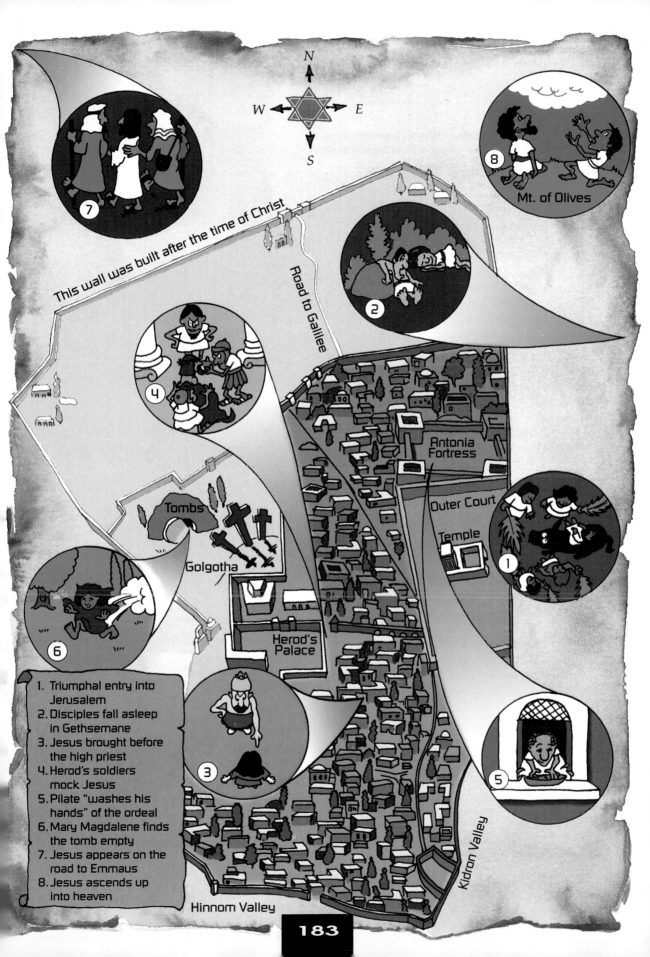

This wall was built after the time of Christ

N
W E
S

Mt. of Olives

Road to Galilee

Antonia
Fortress

Outer Court

Temple

Tombs

Golgotha

Herod's
Palace

Kidron Valley

Hinnom Valley

1. Triumphal entry into
Jerusalem
2. Disciples fall asleep
in Gethsemane
3. Jesus brought before
the high priest
4. Herod's soldiers
mock Jesus
5. Pilate "washes his
hands" of the ordeal
6. Mary Magdalene finds
the tomb empty
7. Jesus appears on the
road to Emmaus
8. Jesus ascends up
into heaven

The Church Begins

Acts

The church in Jerusalem was an exciting place to be. The followers of Jesus (they weren't called "Christians" until a few years later) shared everything they owned with one another, so that nobody had too much or too little to live on.

They prayed together, they sang together, they ate together, and they listened to the apostles (as the disciples were now called) teach about Jesus.

The apostles did many miracles, and the people outside the church were amazed at what was happening. The church didn't have committees or a big building or a television program – but every day new people joined the church because the people in the church were so excited about Jesus and about what he had done for them. *Acts 2:42-47*

For instance, one day Peter and John walked into the court of the temple. There a beggar sat at the entrance every day. But this day, when the man asked for money, Peter said, "I don't have any money, but I will give you what I do have. In the name of Jesus the Messiah, walk!" The man jumped to his feet. Walking and jumping and praising God he went with Peter and John into the temple court. He drew quite a crowd with his excitement and the noise he made, and then Peter and John preached to the crowd. *Acts 3:1-10*

All religious Jews were expected to give money to the poor and the crippled; that is why so many of them gathered in front of the temple to beg.

Check it out! Where are we?

I think it's Solomon's colonnade in Herod's temple.

Awesome.

When Jesus preached, the people loved to listen to him, but the Jewish leaders, especially the Pharisees, had resented him.

Now the people gladly listened to Jesus' followers, but the leaders – this time especially the Sadducees, who didn't believe in a resurrection – hounded the disciples. They arrested Peter and John and put them in jail overnight.

The next day they were brought before all the Jewish leaders, who asked Peter and John where they had gotten the power to heal the crippled beggar. And Peter, a fisherman from Galilee who had never had any schooling, talked without fear to these Jewish leaders and told them that it was Jesus, the One whom they had crucified but whom God had raised from the dead!

The leaders were amazed at Peter's courage. They couldn't deny that something had happened, because the beggar was standing right there. So all they could do was tell Peter and John to quit talking about Jesus.

But Peter and John told the leaders straight out that they would not obey them because God had told them to talk about Jesus! 🐸 *Acts 4:1-22*

Everybody in the church was talking about Jesus to anybody who would listen and soon there were 5,000 followers of Jesus.

The apostles did many miracles, and the church became so big that they had to meet in the only place large enough in all of Jerusalem – a corner of the temple court.

People reacted to the apostles the same way they had reacted to Jesus. They came from all around to hear the apostles speak and brought sick people to be healed. They even laid them on the roadside so that Peter's shadow would fall on them. And all of them were healed. 🌿 *Acts 5:12-16*

The Via Dolorosa, "Street of Suffering," where Jesus probably walked on his way to be crucified.

The Jewish leaders became more and more upset. They put the apostles in prison – but an angel of God let them out, and the next day the apostles were back preaching in the temple. A lot of people listened to the apostles. Even a large number of priests became followers of Jesus!

Finally, things came to a head. One of the followers of Jesus, Stephen, was a powerful preacher who performed many miracles. The leaders didn't like what Stephen did, so they did the same thing with him as they had done with Jesus: They found men who were willing to lie about Stephen and accuse him of insulting God and Moses.

When the Supreme Court asked Stephen if those accusations were true, Stephen preached a long and beautiful sermon. He showed the court how in the past the leaders of Israel had again and again tried to get rid of the prophets and the people who spoke for God. And, Stephen said, "You are doing the very same thing!"

The Jewish leaders got so mad that they dragged Stephen outside the city and stoned him – they threw rocks at him until he died. But as he died Stephen prayed, like Jesus had prayed on the cross: "Lord Jesus, receive my spirit" and "Lord, do not hold this sin against them." He forgave his enemies as he was dying.

One of the people who watched Stephen being stoned was a young Pharisee named Saul, who held people's robes so they could throw better. Saul was glad that Stephen was being stoned. He didn't know yet that God had a big surprise in store for him – many years later people would try to stone him to death because he himself was preaching Jesus. (We know Saul better by his Latin name, Paul.) *Acts 6:8-7:1; 7:51-8:1*

Saul had the same name as Israel's first king, and they both came from the tribe of Benjamin.

187

Saul's Conversion

Acts

The stoning of Stephen was the beginning of a difficult time. The Jewish leaders made life as miserable as possible for the followers of Jesus and put many of them in jail.

As a result, many of Jesus' followers left Jerusalem and went to live in other towns in Judea and Samaria. They took the good news of Jesus with them so that people outside Jerusalem now began to hear about Jesus and about his death and resurrection! 🐸 *Acts 8:1-3*

When Saul heard that quite a few Christians had moved to Damascus in Syria (almost 200 miles from Jerusalem), he asked permission to go there to arrest any Christians he could find and to bring them back to Jerusalem and put them in jail. The Jewish leaders gave Saul official permission, and he went on his way to Damascus.

As he was traveling along, suddenly a bright light shone from heaven, and Saul heard a voice that said, "Saul, Saul, why do you persecute me?" And Saul, who had fallen to the ground, said, "Who are you, sir?" It wasn't a dumb question, because Saul really didn't believe that Jesus was alive. But he got the greatest shock of his life when the voice said, "I am Jesus! Get up and go into the city, and you'll be told what you must do."

When Saul got up, he was blind. The man who had come to Damascus to destroy the church was led into the city by the hand. 🐸 *Acts 9:1-8*

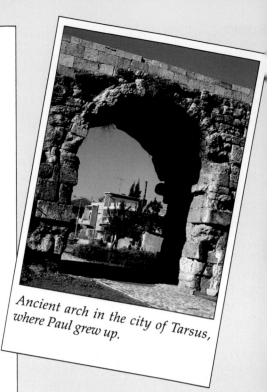

Ancient arch in the city of Tarsus, where Paul grew up.

Saul—the persecutor of Christians

Blinded by the light!

Tertullian, who lived about 150 years after Christ, said, "The blood of the martyrs is the seed of the church." That means that in times of persecution, the church grows and becomes stronger.

Annanias prays for Saul

Group hug everyone! Saul is now
a Christian!

The first non-Jewish person to become a follower of Jesus was a black man from Ethiopia.

Then God told a Christian in Damascus, Ananias, to go to Saul and help him. Ananias wasn't too sure, but God said, "Go! I have chosen this man to preach about me to the people outside Israel and to their kings, and also to the people in Israel. And I will show him how much he will suffer for me." Ananias went, and Saul was able to see again.

Soon Saul went into the synagogues in Damascus, preaching that Jesus is the Son of God! The Jews in Damascus now tried to kill Saul, who had to escape to Jerusalem.

🐸 Acts 9:9-25

The Christians in Jerusalem weren't sure that Saul had really been converted. They thought it was a trick to help Saul discover who the Christians in Jerusalem were, so that he could throw them in jail. But finally one man, Barnabas, convinced the church that Saul was for real, that he had really met Jesus.

So now the Jews in Jerusalem tried to kill Saul. But the church sent Saul to his home town, Tarsus, where he stayed for several years.

🐸 Acts 9:26-31

I hope this doesn't mess up the program!

What are pixels?

The little dots that make up electronic pictures.

Taking out these pixels may help us bypass the invisible wall and get back into full holographic reality.

Peter & Cornelius

Acts

What comes next is difficult for us to understand, but it's very important. The Jews were God's chosen people. God had made covenants (agreements), first with Abraham and then with the people of Israel at Mount Sinai.

The Jews knew that they were special and that God loved them in a special way. They knew that the Messiah would be a Jew and that he would come for his people, the people of Israel. God had not made a covenant with the rest of the people in this world (the Jews called anyone who was not a Jew a "Gentile").

But the Jews hadn't been listening very carefully to the prophets, and the disciples hadn't been listening very carefully to Jesus. The prophets had said that the Messiah would not just come for Israel but for the whole world.

What happened?

Oh no! We're in the control box!

Hang on! I'll crawl down to the keys and fix it!

Gulp! Claustro-froggia.

Until now, the church had been Jewish, and almost all Christians were Jews. Now God had to get across to the church that the message of Jesus was for everybody, whether they were Jews or not.

The church didn't find it easy to understand that. First God had to convince Peter, the leader of the church, that it didn't make any difference whether a person was a Jew or a Greek or a whatever – the followers of Jesus should preach the good news to everybody, because God wanted everybody to know and to believe in Jesus.

One day Peter was sitting on the flat roof of a house in the city of Joppa. He was hungry, and suddenly he saw a large sheet come down from heaven with all kinds of animals. And God said, "Go ahead, Peter, prepare some of these animals and eat." But Peter said, "Surely not, Lord! I have never eaten anything unclean."

Peter didn't mean that the animals were dirty and needed to be washed. The Law of Moses said that some kinds of animals should not be eaten or sacrificed to God. Those were called "unclean" animals. Anybody who ate an unclean animal (a pig, for example) would also be unclean and therefore not please God.

But God said to Peter, "Don't call anything unclean or impure that God has made clean."

It happened three times, and while Peter was still wondering what the vision meant, there was a knock on the door, and two servants of Cornelius, a Roman soldier, asked Peter if he would come and visit Cornelius to talk about Jesus with him. Now, a good Jew would never visit a non-Jew, because the non-Jews were considered "unclean."

Then Peter suddenly realized what the vision meant. The good news of Jesus was for Jews and non-Jews alike. Peter went to Cornelius's house, and while he was talking to Cornelius, the Holy Spirit came to everybody who was listening. Nobody could have any doubt now that the good news of Jesus was for everyone – Jews and non-Jews, men and women, boys and girls! 🐸 *Acts 10:1-35, 44-48*

But the Christians in Jerusalem still weren't sure, so Peter had to tell them what had happened to Cornelius. They were very happy that God also loved other people and not just the Jews. 🐸 *Acts 11:1-18*

Hebrews

We don't know who wrote the letter to the Hebrews, but we know when – probably before the Romans destroyed the temple in Jerusalem in A.D. 70.

The letter is written to Hebrews (Jews) who had become Christians. Now they were being persecuted and thrown in prison – just because they were Christians! They could save their lives and property by rejecting Jesus and going back to the Jewish faith.

This letter tries to convince these Hebrew Christians not to turn their back on Jesus and not to go back to Judaism.

• It shows them again and again how much greater Jesus is than the things of the Old Testament, which were only foreshadowings of Jesus.

• The letter also warns the Hebrew Christians what will happen if they stop believing in Jesus.

• It encourages them by telling them how much God loves them and by reminding them of the stories in the Old Testament about people who received God's help in difficult times.

Hebrews 11:1-40

Eeeek! Worms! Chip, hurry up down there!

Chip, please don't hit the map key! My head can't take any more abuse!

I t had been quiet for the church in Jerusalem for several years. But then King Herod Agrippa decided that he didn't like the Christians, and he began to persecute them.

He killed one of the apostles, James, the brother of John, and he threw Peter in prison. The king would probably have killed Peter too, but the whole church was praying for him. In the middle of the night an angel of God came and told Peter to follow him. And Peter walked with the angel right out of prison.

He went to the house where the church was holding the prayer meeting. The girl who opened the door couldn't believe it was Peter and slammed the door in his face!

Acts 12:1-19

Herod: A King Fit for a Feast

Chow Now!

Herod or bust!

Herod Agrippa

King Herod Agrippa was a grandson of King Herod the Great who had built the new temple. The family of Herod was a mess. Herod the Great had given the order to kill all babies under two years old in Bethlehem.

Herod Agrippa's uncle, Herod Antipas, had beheaded John the Baptist and given John's head on a platter to his daughter, Salome.

Herod Agrippa's father had been killed by his own father, Herod the Great. Not a nice family.

Herod Agrippa himself died when the people tried to tell him that he was a god. The Bible says that "he was eaten by worms and died."

Matthew 14:1-12 *Acts 12:1-14; 19b-23*

Coin with head of Herod Agrippa.

Peter was the leader of the church in Jerusalem until he got out of prison. Then he became a missionary, and the leadership of the church was turned over to James, one of Jesus' brothers.

Paul earned his own money as a missionary by making tents.

I told you not to hit the map key!

Hang in there, Brad!

Paul's First Trip

Acts

SYRIA

Antioch

Seleucia Pieria ①

CYPRUS

Salamis

② Paphos

Mediterranean Sea

Jerusalem

PAMPHYLIA

Antioch

Derbe

Iconium

Lystra

Perga ④

Attalia

Antioch ③

Lystra: Paul is stoned and dragged out of town. ④

Antioch: Paul brings the gospel to the gentiles. ③

Selucia Pieria: the trip begins. ①

Cyprus: Elymas the sorcerer goes blind. ②

W hile the church was being persecuted in Jerusalem, Paul was in Antioch, about 350 miles north of Jerusalem. Barnabas, the man who had convinced the church that Paul had really become a follower of Jesus and who had helped Paul escape to Tarsus when the Jews in Jerusalem wanted to kill him, had gone to Tarsus so Paul could go with him to Antioch.

There the followers of Jesus were called "Christians" for the first time. From then on that is what everybody called them.

When Paul and Barnabas had been in Antioch for a whole year, God told the church in Antioch to send Paul and Barnabas on a long trip to preach the gospel. Paul didn't know it yet, but this would be only the first of at least three long trips. These trips are called "missionary journeys" because Paul was really the first missionary to foreign countries.

This first trip wasn't too terribly long – about 1,400 miles. It took about a year and a half. Paul and Barnabas went to the island of Cyprus in the Mediterranean Sea, where a sorcerer named Elymas tried to keep them from talking to the governor of the island. Paul got very angry, and he said, "You are a child of the devil and an enemy of everything that is right!" And he told Elymas that he would be blind for a while. When Elymas did go blind, the governor became a Christian. *Acts 13:1-12*

The two kept traveling and preaching, but wherever they went, the Jews worked against them. For instance, they came to Lystra, where Paul healed a man who had been crippled all his life. When the crowd saw what Paul had done, they actually thought that Paul and Barnabas were gods: they thought that Paul was Zeus, the most important Greek god, and Barnabas was Hermes, Zeus' messenger. (You can recognize Hermes in ancient pictures because he wears funny shoes with wings.)

Even when Paul and Barnabas told the people that they really were not that they really were not Zeus and Hermes, the people still wanted to bring them sacrifices – they had a bull ready to be killed and sacrificed to them!

But then the Jews who had followed Paul and Barnabas to Lystra began to talk to the crowd and convinced them that Paul and Barnabas were evil men. So the same people who had wanted to make them gods got mad and stoned Paul – just like the people who wanted to make Jesus king a week later yelled, "Crucify him!"

But the Christians in Lystra all came and stood in a circle around Paul, and Paul got up and went back into the city. The next day Paul and Barnabas traveled on. In some cities there were already Christians, so they not only preached but also appointed elders in those churches, people who could lead the churches. *Acts 14:8-20*

I can't see anything!

Over here, Rebecca!

I've found the blitz key! Hang on!

The Meeting in Jerusalem

Acts

At first, the church's problems came from the outside, from people who didn't want to hear about Jesus. But soon there was a problem *inside* the church.

You remember how God showed Peter that the gospel was for everybody, whether they were Jews or not. But some Jewish Christians said, yes, the gospel is for everybody, but anyone who is not a Jew must first become a Jew – they must first be circumcised and keep all the other laws of Moses, and then they can become Christians.

Because many Christians were confused, all the apostles came to Jerusalem for a meeting. Peter and James (Jesus' brother), were in charge of the meeting. First Peter spoke: "Listen! God saves Jews and Gentiles alike. We know, because he gives the Holy Spirit to all, whether they are Jews or not! People are saved by the grace of the Lord Jesus, not by keeping the Law of Moses!"

And Paul and Barnabas told what they had seen God do as they were traveling: People were saved, even if they hadn't been circumcised or kept Moses' Law.

Finally James spoke. He said, "Let's write a letter, telling everybody that Christians do not have to become Jews first. There are a few things they should not do, not because the Law says they can't do them but because these things are done in the worship of idols, for example, eating blood." And they sent a letter to the churches explaining their decision.

Acts 15:1-21

Oh, oh. Looks like we interrupted an important theological discussion!

The blitz didn't work. What do we do now?

If we work together, we can type a command to the computer.

Thousands of old Greek letters written on papyrus have been found in Egypt; many of them begin with the same kind of greeting as the letters in the Bible.

Writing Letters

Thirteen of the twenty letters in the New Testament were written by the apostle Paul.

If the people in one of the churches had an important question, they would send someone from the church to visit Paul, or they would write him a letter. And Paul would write a letter to answer such questions as:

• Do we have to become Jews to be saved?
• Do we have to do good works to be saved?
• When is Jesus going to return?
• What should we do with people who say they believe in Jesus but don't live like it?

Paul also wrote letters to encourage people to keep on being Christians – even when they were persecuted. He often reminded them how much Jesus suffered for them.

It's easy to send a letter to someone today. But 2,000 years ago there weren't any mailboxes or post offices. The Roman Empire had a postal service, but it could only be used for official government letters. It was very difficult to get a letter to a friend or a family member.

For example, if you lived in Ephesus and wanted to send a letter to a friend in Rome, you'd have to find someone who was going to Rome, and you would have to make sure that that person knew how to find your friend in Rome. That could be difficult, since people didn't have addresses as we do today.

The only sure way to get a letter to a friend was to give it to someone who knew both you and your friend. And that's the way most of the letters in the New Testament were delivered.

In Paul's day, letters were written on sheets made from papyrus leaves, with ink and a pen made from a hollow stalk of reed (a kind of grass), sharpened at one end into a point.

Paul did not write his own letters. Instead, he dictated them to someone who wrote them down. See Romans 16:22 to find the name of the "writer" of Romans!

This scroll is almost exactly like the one Jesus read from (Luke 4:16-20).

Galatians

The apostle Paul wrote this letter to the churches in Galatia probably in the same year that the Jerusalem Conference was held, and he wrote about the same problem that was talked about at the conference: Some people in the church said that anybody who wasn't born a Jew should become a Jew first before he or she could become a Christian.

Paul uses very strong language to tell the churches in Galatia that the people who say that you have to become a Jew before you can become a Christian are not preaching the gospel of Jesus at all, but an entirely different gospel – they are condemned! 🐸 *Galatians 1:6-10*

All that matters is that we trust God and believe that Jesus has made things right between God and us. It doesn't make any difference what color our skin is or what language we speak or how smart we are. 🐸 *Galatians 3:26-29*

And when we trust God, the Holy Spirit will work in our lives to make us more like Jesus. 🐸 *Galatians 5:22-26*

Paul didn't write his letters himself. Like most people in those days, he dictated them to someone who would write down exactly what he said. At the end of each letter, Paul usually wrote a few words himself, using great big letters (maybe because his eyesight was bad). These last few words in Paul's own handwriting showed that the letter really came from Paul. 🐸 *Galatians 6:11-18*

Paul

When the letters of Paul were collected, they were placed in order of length, not in the order in which they were written.

1 and 2 Peter

Peter

The Bible doesn't tell us what happened to Peter after the Jerusalem Conference, but we do have two of the letters he wrote.

Of all of Jesus' disciples, Peter was the one who most often did and said things before thinking about them – he was a hot-head. (Read, for example, John 18:10-11.) But when Peter wrote his letters he was much older and had become much wiser and mellower.

He had learned that God works differently (and sometimes much more slowly) than we would like.

Peter's first letter is for Christians who are being persecuted and often killed – just because they are Christians.
🐸 *1 Peter 1:6-9*

If things get difficult, remember that we didn't choose God – God chose us! And the way to "fight back" is to live as God's children should – like Jesus! 🐸 *1 Peter 2:9-25;* 🐸 *1 Peter 3:8-12*

And when you remember how easily Peter would fly off the handle, you can see how much Peter changed when he talks about how to react when you are given a hard time because you do what is right instead of giving in to peer pressure.
🐸 *1 Peter 3:13-17*

Peter also talks about what will happen at the end of time.
🐸 *2 Peter 3:8-13*

This adds new meaning to "the letters of Paul"!

Type this: E-N-L-A-R-G-E T-O-O-N-S. B-I -I-T-Z. O-U-T.

So much for my typing 60 words per minute.

By the time Peter wrote his second letter, the letters of Paul were becoming popular reading for Christians everywhere (see 2 Peter 3:15-16).

Two letters in the New Testament were written by brothers of Jesus: James and Jude. At first they didn't believe that Jesus was the Messiah, but later they became his followers. James was a leader in the church and spoke at the Jerusalem Conference.
John 7:1-5   *Acts 15:12-21*

Nice blitz for a change.

What a relief to get out of that box.

James

James

James is very practical. His letter tells us that if we really believe in Jesus and have his love in our hearts, we won't pretend to be his followers by saying all the right things (the things we think people want to hear), but we will do what Jesus says we should do. (James reminds us that Satan believes everything the Bible says about Jesus – but Satan does the opposite of what God wants.)

• You can go to church and listen to sermons all your life, but if you ignore the things God tells you to do, you're kidding yourself!
James 1:19-27

• Faith that is only in your brain and never makes a bit of difference in your everyday life is no faith at all.
James 2:14-26

• Watch what you say and don't say!
James 3:1-12 – especially 9-12

Jude

Jude

Jude started to write a cheerful letter – until he heard that some people in the church were teaching wrong things about Christ. So he wrote a strong, harsh leter of warning instead.

But the last thing Jude says in his letter is very beautiful, and you have probably heard it many times (it's sometimes called a "doxology"). *Jude 24-25*

Look! A spelling mistake!

How could the proofreader have missed that? We better have a talk with our publisher!

Paul's Second Trip

Acts

The church council in Jerusalem was over, and Paul had gone back to Antioch, where he wrote to the Galatians. But sometimes it is better to talk with people than to write to them, so Paul decided to do both and visit the churches in Galatia as well.

And as long as he was traveling anyway, he might as well visit some other places. Paul didn't plan it this way, but this trip (usually called the second missionary journey) turned out to be twice as long as his first trip (about 2,800 miles) and took two years.

Paul traveled with Silas instead of Barnabas (Paul and Barnabas had had a disagreement), and they picked up a third companion: Timothy, a young man who would become one of Paul's closest friends and helpers.

The first part of the trip through Galatia was uneventful. But when they came to Troas on the shore of the Aegean Sea, Paul had a dream: A man from Macedonia, the country right across the sea from Troas, was begging Paul, "Come over to Macedonia and help us!"
Acts 16:1-10

Paul probably traveled by foot or by mule, covering about twenty miles per day.

So Paul, Silas, and Timothy crossed the sea and landed in Europe, where the first big city they came to was Philippi. And as quiet as the first part of the trip had been, so exciting did things get in Philippi. The first person to become a Christian in Philippi was Lydia, a business-woman. ⚓ *Acts 16:11-15*

So far so good. But one day Paul and Silas ran into a slave girl who had an evil spirit that helped her predict the future. She pointed at Paul and Silas and shouted, "These men are servants of the Most High God, who are telling you the way to be saved!" And she did this every day, for a long time, until Paul finally turned around and told the evil spirit in the name of Jesus Christ to come out of the girl. And, of course, the spirit left her.

But now she could no longer make money for her owners through fortune telling. Her owners wanted revenge. They accused Paul and Silas of teaching things that went against the law.

Paul and Silas were beaten and thrown in jail. In jail, Paul and Silas prayed and sang hymns! Suddenly, a violent earthquake shook the building, the prison doors flew open, and everybody's chains fell off.

Under Roman law a jailer who lost his prisoners also lost his life. So when the jailer saw that the doors of the jail were open, he thought that the jail was empty and decided that he'd rather be dead now than executed later.

But Paul said, "Don't hurt yourself – we're all here!" And when Paul and Silas told him the good news of Jesus, the jailer and his family became Christians.

The next day the city council sent someone to the jail to tell the jailer that Paul and Silas were free to go. But Paul and Silas said, "No way! You beat us in public, without a trial, and you threw us in prison. But we are Roman citizens, and we demand that the city council come here in person and escort us out of prison."

Lystra: Timothy joins Paul and becomes his faithful companion.

(1)

Adriatic Sea

I T A L Y

Philippi was located on the most important road in the eastern part of the Roman Empire, the Via Egnatia.

Troas: Paul has a vision of a man calling him to come over to Macedonia.

(2)

Philippi: Paul stops the jailer from killing himself.

(3)

The city council was scared. They hadn't realized that Paul and Silas were Roman citizens (they hadn't asked!) and Roman law was very strict – a Roman citizen could not be beaten and sent to prison without a trial. So the city council came to the jail and very humbly asked Paul and Silas if they would please leave the city – which they did, and the city council breathed a collective sigh of relief. *Acts 16:16-40*

The city of Philippi did not have a synagogue, so the Jews who lived there prayed every Sabbath at a place by the river.

Corinth: Paul begins writing letters to other churches. ⑦

MACEDONIA

Philippi ③
Neapolis
Thessalonica
Berea ④
Amphipolis
Apollonia
Troas ②

BITHYNIA

GALATIA

Antioch
Iconium
Lystra ①
Derbe
Tarsus

CILICIA

ASIA

Ephesus

Athens ⑤
Corinth ⑦

⑥

Where's all the stuff?

Didn't that shopkeeper sound familiar?

Chip, are you sure you told the control box to blitz our gear?

Come on! I want to see Paul trash those Greek philosophers in a debate!

CRETE

CYPRUS

SYRIA

Antioch

Mediterranean Sea

Caesarea
Jerusalem

Thessalonica: a mob attacks the house of Jason where Paul is staying. ④

Athens: Paul talks with Epicurean and Stoic philosophers. ⑤

Tracy, Chip, Brad, Rebecca, and Jay 100 miles from Athens with no equipment. ⑥

As the church kept growing, the Jews became more jealous of the Christians. In Thessalonica, quite a few people became Christians, but the Jews there started a riot and blamed Paul and Silas, so they had to leave the city. 🐸 *Acts 17:1-9*

In the next city, Berea, the Jews took Paul's message seriously and many believed. But the Jews from Thessalonica came to Berea and again tried to start a riot. So Paul had to leave again, this time going to Athens. 🐸 *Acts 17:10-15*

In Athens, Paul saw that there were many statues of all kinds of gods. The Athenians were so afraid of overlooking a god and making that unknown god mad by not worshiping him that they even put up an altar "To an Unknown God."

So Paul went up to the Areopagus, the place where all the philosophers met, and said, "I saw an altar 'To an Unknown God' in your city – and I am going to tell you about that unknown God." And he preached to them about Jesus and how God had raised him from the dead, but not too many Athenians believed Paul.
🐸 *Acts 17:16-34*

When Paul got to the next city, Corinth, he took a break from traveling and stayed for a year and a half, preaching and writing letters. We still have two of the letters Paul wrote from Corinth; they were both written to the church in Thessalonica, the city where the Jews had started a big riot so that Paul and Silas had to leave.

From Corinth, Paul and Silas traveled back to Antioch, stopping briefly in Jerusalem.

Stoics were philosophers who believed that wise people should not feel pleasure or pain.

When Paul first saw the Parthenon (the temple on top of the hill) in Athens, it was already more than 500 years old. In 1687, somebody was stupid enough to store gunpowder in it, and it blew up.

1 and 2 Thessalonians

Paul 🐸 *Acts 17:1-9*

When Paul started the church in Thessalonica, he only had a few weeks to teach the new Christians before he was thrown out of the city.

One of the things Paul had not yet talked about to the Thessalonians was what happens after a Christian dies. Paul heard from his friend Timothy that the Christians in Thessalonica were very sad because some of their friends were dying. They thought that that was the end of them.

So Paul wrote this letter to tell them that Jesus is coming back and that Christians who die have really only "fallen asleep," since they will be raised back to life when Jesus returns! 🐸 *1 Thessalonians 4:13-18*

But people sometimes hear a wonderful truth and come to wrong conclusions. After the people in Thessalonica read Paul's first letter, some of them said, "Oh well, if Jesus is coming back anyway, why should I worry about my job or about my school work – I may as well enjoy the time until Jesus comes back!"

So these people quit their jobs, even though they were supposed to be providing food for themselves and their families. And it didn't take too long before they ran out of money and couldn't afford to buy food any more. So they started bothering other members of the church and begging for food.

When Timothy came to Paul in Corinth and told him this, Paul wrote his second letter to the Thessalonians. He told them that Jesus would not return until after the Antichrist appeared. And because the Antichrist had not yet appeared, it would be a while before Jesus returned.
🐸 *2 Thessalonians 2:1-4*

Therefore, Paul said, go back to work and be responsible people! Work and do the best you can.
🐸 *2 Thessalonians 3:6-15*

Each of the five chapters of 1 Thessalonians ends with a reference to the second coming of Christ.

PHILOSOPHIC DELICATESSEN

UNKNOWN MEAT

SPECIAL

LAMB

Hmm, bad turban day.

Mmm.

Froggo's Plate o' Play-Dough Plato!

Me next, Brad!

Epicureans were philosophers who lived for feelings of pleasure. Their motto today would be "If it feels good, do it!"

Try our delicious food for thought! Our tough meat is perfect for the stoic. For the epicurean, we have lovely spiced lamb. And our special today, for just **$9.99** – unknown meat! We don't know where it came from or what it is, but we've got it, just in case!

Paul's Third Trip

Acts

The temple to the goddess Diana in Ephesus was four times larger than the Parthenon in Athens (see page 204).

Paul made a third long trip, almost as long as his last one. On this third missionary journey Paul traveled about 2,700 miles in four years.

He went back to some of the churches in Galatia and in Asia Minor (what is now called Turkey). One of the cities Paul went to was Ephesus, where there was a beautiful temple for the goddess Diana (also known as Artemis). Not only were the people of Ephesus proud of their temple, they made a lot of money from people who came to visit it and bought small silver models of the temple.

When Paul preached about Jesus, one of the silver smiths, Demetrius, was afraid that his business would be ruined if too many people believed in Jesus, so he started a riot. The whole city went to the theater (you can still see the ruins today), even though many people had no idea why they were rioting. Fortunately, the city clerk was able to calm the crowd, and Paul was able to move on.

🐸 *Acts 19:23-41*

In Troas, just before going across the water to Philippi, Paul talked to the church – until midnight. One young man, Eutychus, did what you never should do when you're sitting in an open window on the third floor: He fell asleep and out of the window. The fall killed Eutychus, but Paul raised him from the dead – and then kept talking until daybreak (and you think your church services are long!).

🐸 *Acts 20:7-12*

Paul went on to Philippi and Corinth. On the way back he stopped again in Ephesus to say good-by to the church there. Paul knew that at the end of this trip, when he reached Jerusalem, things would be very difficult and he probably would end up in prison – which is, of course, what happened.

🐸 *Acts 20:22-24*

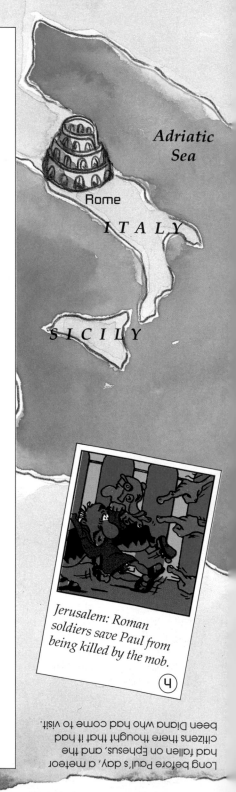

Adriatic Sea

Rome

I T A L Y

S I C I L Y

Jerusalem: Roman soldiers save Paul from being killed by the mob.

④

Long before Paul's day, a meteor had fallen on Ephesus, and the citizens there thought that it had been Diana who had come to visit.

Ephesus: Demetrius blames Paul for ruining his goddess-making business. ①

Sometimes Paul gets very tired and weak, but see 2 Corinthians 12:9–10. ②

Philippi: a young man nods off and falls out of a window while Paul talks. ③

Many new Christians in Ephesus had a big bonfire of all the books they owned about black magic and demon worship.

MACEDONIA

Philippi ③
Neapolis
Troas
Assos
Mitylene

GREECE

Corinth

PHRYGIA

GALATIA

Antioch
Iconium
Lystra
Derbe
Tarsus

CILICIA

① Ephesus
Miletus

PAMPHYLIA

Patara

RHODES

CRETE

Antioch

SYRIA

CYPRUS

Mediterranean Sea

Ptolegmais
Tyre
Caesarea ⑤
Jerusalem
④

Caesarea: Paul is taken to Caesarea by Roman soldiers and cavalry. ⑤

Tracy, Chip, Brad, Rebecca, and Jay under this map, between the pages. ⑥

That was Max! I know it was! Him and his $9.99's

BUMP! BUMP!
BUMP!

Where are we?

⑥

I think the control box confused our report with holographic reality. We're under the pages of our report!

1 and 2 Corinthians

Paul

Christians aren't perfect people. And because the church is made up of imperfect people, there aren't any perfect churches either. The church in Corinth was not even close to perfect. There were huge problems. People argued and disagreed with each other. Some people were so angry that they would hardly talk to others who sat next to them in church. There was immorality in the church, people got drunk at the Lord's Supper, and the church services in Corinth were chaotic.

In his first letter to the Corinthians, Paul told them that their arguments were unimportant when compared with the wonderful things they had in common: They all loved Jesus, and God had given the church in Corinth marvelous gifts.

He said, just as your body has a lot of different parts, so the church has many different kinds of people – some smart, some not so smart, some good-looking, some ugly, some nice, some not so nice – but they all belong together in one body (the church).
🐸 *1 Corinthians 12:12-31*

The most important thing he told them was that there was only one way for all the different people in the church to get along – they had to learn to love each other.
🐸 *1 Corinthians 13:1-13*

This is the great chapter about love. If you think it isn't very practical, read how it applies to your life:

- Love will stand in line and wait its turn.
- Love looks for the good things in others.
- Love doesn't always want what others have, and it doesn't brag about what it does have.

The very first letter Paul wrote to the church in Corinth is now lost. Apparently it didn't contain anything that is important for us to know.

- Love is polite, even when the other person is rude.
- Love doesn't always have to be first.
- Love doesn't get angry over the small things, and it doesn't remember the times it was hurt by other people.
- Love isn't happy when someone else fails but is happy with the truth.
- Love will always protect others, especially those who are often picked on or teased.
- Love always believes the best about others and is steady and true.

There was also wrong teaching in the church at Corinth. Some people said that there was no resurrection of the dead, but Paul shows that if those people are right, Christianity is a lie.

1 Corinthians 15:3-8, 12-19

After the Corinthians read Paul's first letter they stopped fighting, right? Wrong! In fact, the fighting got even worse. It made Paul feel so bad that he made a quick visit to Corinth to see if the people would listen to him in person. But that didn't work either.

Finally Paul sent his good friend Titus. With God's help, Titus found a way to get the Christians in Corinth to stop fighting, to listen to Paul, and to love each other again.

Paul was so excited when he heard that the problems in Corinth were over that he wrote them another letter – 2 Corinthians. It is one of his happiest and most excited letters. He thanks God over and over for solving the problems in the church in Corinth.

And since Paul had heard that many of the Christians in Jerusalem didn't have enough food to eat, he asked the Christians in Corinth and in other places to help them with money to buy food. Paul encouraged them to be generous with the things God had given them. *2 Corinthians 9:6-15*

Greek has a verb "korinthiazo," which means "to live like a resident of Corinth," or, in other words, "to live a very sinful life"!

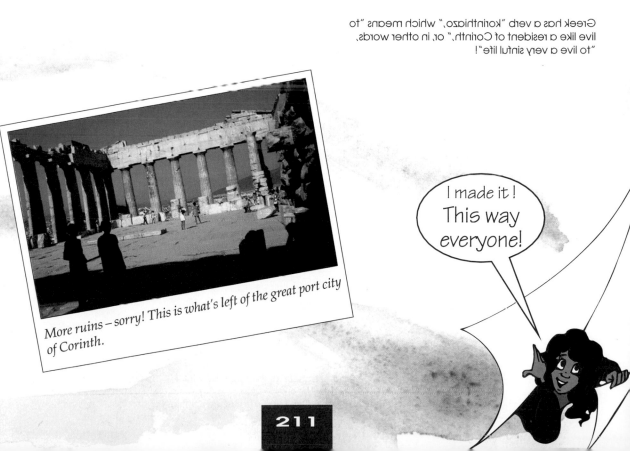

More ruins – sorry! This is what's left of the great port city of Corinth.

I made it! This way everyone!

Romans

Paul

The apostle Paul wrote this letter to the Christians in Rome, the capital of the Roman Empire, the largest empire the world had ever seen. Rome was a wonderful city to live in – if you were rich. But most people in Rome were poor, and more than half of the one million people in Rome were slaves.

When Paul wrote this letter, Nero was emperor of Rome. He was a cruel man who had murdered his own mother! Seven years after Paul wrote his letter to the Romans, a fire broke out in one of the slums in Rome and destroyed half the city. Soon there were rumors that Nero himself had set the fire to make room for new building projects. Nero decided to blame the Christians, and that is when the persecution of the Christians really began. Many Christians were killed just because they were Christians.

The letter to the Romans is not the easiest book of the Bible to read. But it is a wonderful book because Paul tells the Romans exactly what the gospel is all about.

Everybody, no matter how good they may seem, has sinned and disobeyed God. 🐸 *Romans 1:18-23*

🐸 *Romans 3:23*

How can we be accepted by God? Not by keeping the Law of Moses or any other set of rules. No matter how hard we try, we'll always end up doing wrong things.

🐸 *Romans 2:12*

The only way for us to have a relationship to God is to accept God's righteousness, simply by believing that Jesus died in our place! There is nothing else we can do to be reconciled with God.

🐸 *Romans 3:21-24*
🐸 *Romans 5:10-11*

When we believe in Jesus, will we suddenly be perfect? In God's eyes, yes. But we will still do wrong things, as Paul well knew. He certainly wasn't perfect.

🐸 *Romans 7:15, 19, 24-25*

So what happens then? The best news of all is that nothing – not even sin – can ever separate us from God again!

🐸 *Romans 8:1-2, 26-39*

In the last part of most of his letters Paul gives guidelines for living as Christians, and he does that also in this letter. For example, one very practical thing he says is that we shouldn't make fun of or look down on people who aren't as good at something as we are, or as smart or good-looking; we must treat them the way we would want to be treated if we were klutzy or not so smart or good-looking!

🐸 *Romans 15:1, 7*

Jay! I've got it! Max is some sort of glitch in the computer program!

Give us our money back, you electronic scoundrel!

Calm down, Jay!

Hey, guys!
Forget Max! Let's go over the page!

Inside the Colosseum in Rome. The rooms you see were under the floor of the arena. In these rooms the gladiators, lions, and Christians waited until they had to go into the arena to fight and be killed.

The Mamertine prison in Rome, where Paul is supposed to have spent the last years of his life.

The arch of Titus in Rome built in honor of the general who conquered Judea and destroyed Jerusalem in A.D. 70. Titus later became emperor of Rome.

Me?
You talking about me? Whatsamatter? I'm just Max, the merchant!

Paul's Arrest

Acts

After his third trip, Paul went back to Jerusalem. He told the apostles and the rest of the church the great things God had done during his travels.

But the apostles were worried that when the Jews found out that Paul was in Jerusalem, they would cause trouble. And they were right.

Some Jews from Asia Minor saw Paul preaching and started a big uproar by falsely accusing Paul of speaking against the Law and the temple, and of bringing Greeks into the temple (which was, of course, strictly forbidden).

It got so out of hand that the crowd was ready to kill Paul. He was rescued by Roman soldiers, who were stationed in the Antonia fortress that was built right next to the temple.

After the Romans arrested Paul, the commander tried to figure out why the Jews were so mad at Paul. But the commander couldn't make heads nor tails out of what was going on, so he ordered Paul to be taken to the barracks – the mob was so wild that the soldiers had to carry Paul to get him through the crowd! *Acts 21:27-36*

Paul asked for permission to talk to the crowd from the steps of the barracks, but that only made things worse. The people yelled, "Rid the earth of him! He is not fit to live!" *Acts 21:37-22:22*

The commander then ordered Paul to be whipped and questioned, but when the soldiers stood ready with the whip, Paul said, "Is it legal for you to whip a Roman citizen who hasn't been tried and found guilty?" *Acts 22:23-29*

Paul planned to do mission work in Spain and to visit the church in Rome on the way there. We don't know whether he ever made it to Spain.

214

That gave the commander a scare, and he released Paul and invited the Sanhedrin to come and question Paul. So Paul (protected by Roman soldiers) stood before the Sanhedrin.

Until then, the whole uproar had been caused by the Jews, who wanted to get rid of Paul. But standing before the Sanhedrin, it was Paul who created a major disturbance. Paul knew full well that there were two parties in the Sanhedrin: the Pharisees, who believed that there was life after death, and the Sadducees, who didn't believe in life after death. So Paul said, "I am standing here because of my hope in the resurrection of the dead!" And the two groups of scholars and leaders began to fight among themselves – and not just with words. Things got so hot that the Roman commander decided he'd better take Paul away before the two parties tore him to pieces!

Acts 22:30-23:11

Model of Jerusalem in the time of Christ, viewed from the southwest. The temple is in the background. To the left of the temple, with the four square towers, is the Antonia fortress where Jesus stood before Pilate and where Paul was taken by the Romans.

When Paul spoke to the Romans, he spoke in Greek (or maybe even Latin); when he spoke to the Jews, he spoke in Aramaic (which was like Hebrew).

What did I do?
What did I do?

It's bad enough that I fall on my head. Do you have to fall on it too?

Sorry, Brad

I need a doctor.

A doctor! That's it! Max is a computer virus! I'll create a disk doctor program that will fix him!

Now you're talking.

But the Jews still wanted to kill Paul. They were planning to ask the Romans to bring Paul again before the Sanhedrin, and on the way to the meeting they would ambush and kill him.

But Paul's nephew heard about the plot and told the Roman commander about it. The commander sent Paul to the Roman governor in Caesarea, a city built by Herod the Great and named after the emperor, Caesar. (The people who wanted to kill Paul had sworn that they would not eat or drink until they killed Paul. If they kept their vow, they must have died of starvation.)

Acts 23:12-35

Paul was brought before Felix, the governor, who listened to the accusations against Paul. He knew in his heart that Paul was not guilty. But he didn't set Paul free. Instead, he hoped that Paul would offer him a bribe. When Paul didn't, Felix kept him waiting – for two years.

Acts 24:24-27

Here we go… I've typed in the list of commands… do's and don'ts, cans and can'ts, laws and rules and so forth…

What's up, Doc?

Hey, there. Dr. Mo here. Dr. Mo says take two stone tablets and call me in the morning…

Felix was no longer allowed to govern the Jews because he had done such a poor job of handling riots.

Then Felix was replaced by a new governor, Festus. Since Festus was new, he wanted to get on the good side of the Jews. "Why not send Paul back to Jerusalem," he thought. But Paul knew that if that happened the Jews would surely kill him. So Paul made use of his right as a Roman citizen to appeal to the Roman supreme court, to the emperor himself. 🦋 *Acts 25:1-12*

This meant that now nobody except the emperor in Rome had the right to try Paul's case. And even though Governor Festus and King Agrippa both agreed that Paul should really be set free, it was too late – Paul had to go to Rome.

But the two years in Caesarea were not wasted. Paul was able to talk about Jesus and the gospel to the Roman soldiers, to two Roman governors, and to King Herod Agrippa.

Weird.

Go, Mo!

Hey, Chip, another map's coming up. Can we use this rope instead of blitzing?

Dr. Mo seems to be doing the trick!

Dr. Mo says you are an evil little virus. He say, "Come here, you naughty little man. I will operate on your bad sectors!"

*No, no. I **beg** you. I can't stand needles!*

I hope your parents aren't offended, but I wanted to show you this picture to prove that Bible characters are real people, too. You guessed it – it's an ancient rest room in Philippi. Must have been awfully cold in winter!

The city of Caesarea has some of the best preserved ruins of buildings in all the ancient world.

Paul's Trip to Rome

Acts

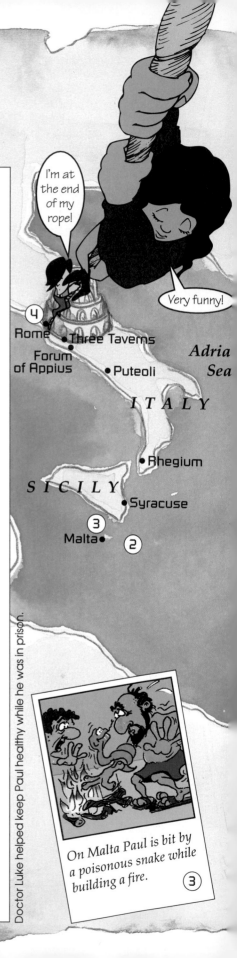

I'm at the end of my rope!

Very funny!

Paul almost didn't make it to Rome. The fastest way to get to Rome was by ship, so Paul and his Roman guard, as well as Doctor Luke (who wrote the gospel of Luke and the book of Acts) set out on a ship across the Mediterranean Sea.

The first part of the trip was easy, because the ship could stay close to the shore. But when they tried to cross over to Cyprus, stiff winds slowed them down, and they arrived on Cyprus much later than expected.

And now they had to go across the open sea to Malta – about 400 miles, which wasn't bad in the summer months but was dangerous in October, when there could be severe storms. Paul warned the people on the ship that they would be shipwrecked if they sailed on from Cyprus to Malta. But they ignored Paul.

And sure enough, they were caught by the winds and were blown across the sea for almost 600 miles, far from land. All 276 people aboard the ship were terrified, but Paul promised that no one would get hurt – only the ship would be destroyed.

And that's what happened. The ship ran aground on a sand bar in sight of the coast of the island of Malta. Those who could swim, swam ashore, and the rest grabbed planks from the boat (which was smashed to pieces by the waves) and floated ashore.

It was raining and cold on Malta, and they built a fire to keep warm. But when Paul picked up some fire wood, there was a poisonous snake in it that bit Paul's hand. Everybody expected Paul to swell up or suddenly fall dead, but nothing happened – so the islanders thought that he was a god. Of course, Paul told them he wasn't; he preached the gospel and healed many sick people.

Acts 27:1-28:10

Doctor Luke helped keep Paul healthy while he was in prison.

Rome ④
Three Taverns
Forum of Appius
Puteoli

Adria Sea

ITALY

Rhegium

SICILY

Syracuse

Malta ③ ②

On Malta Paul is bit by a poisonous snake while building a fire.
③

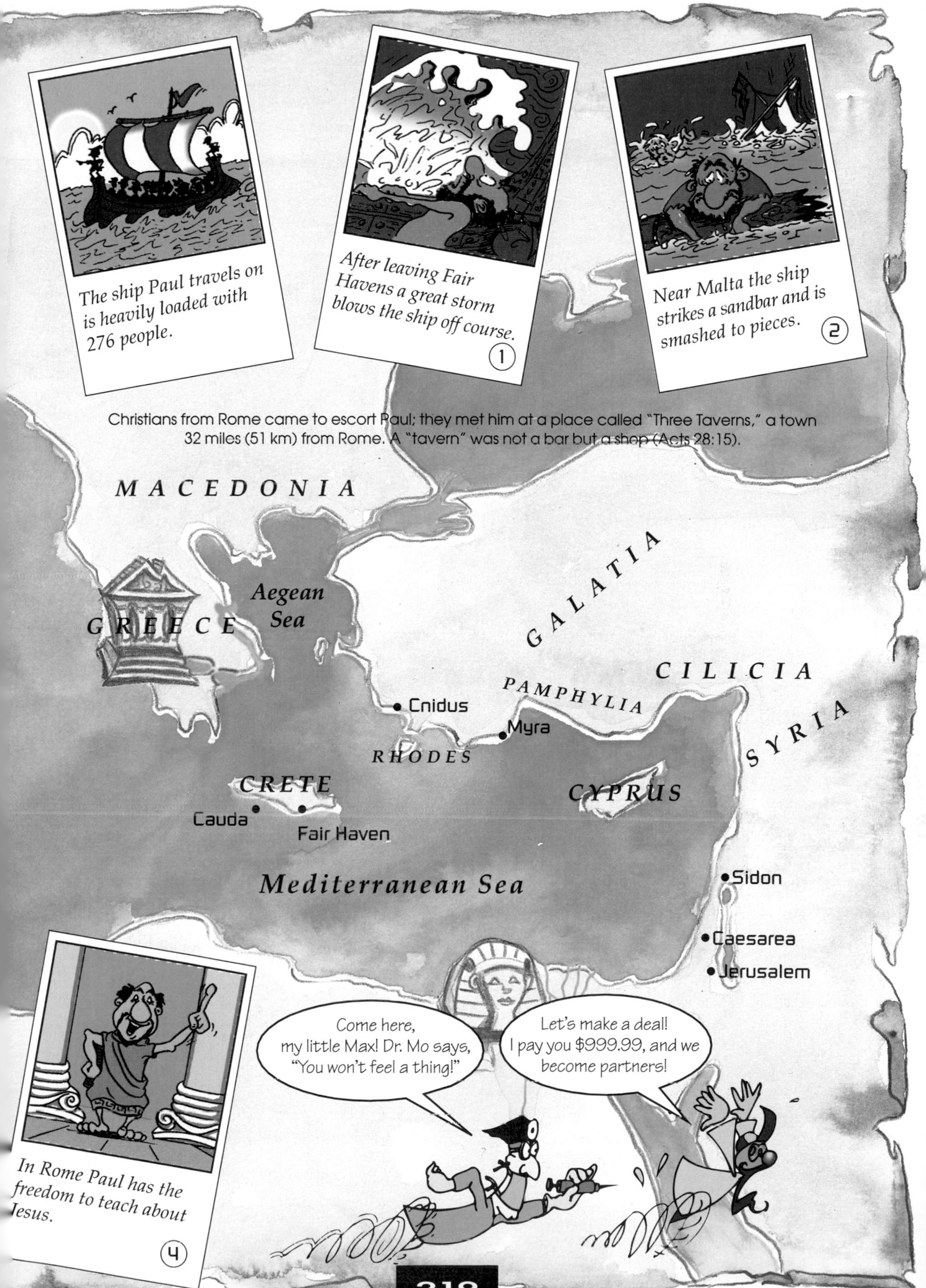

The ship Paul travels on is heavily loaded with 276 people.

After leaving Fair Havens a great storm blows the ship off course.
①

Near Malta the ship strikes a sandbar and is smashed to pieces.
②

Christians from Rome came to escort Paul; they met him at a place called "Three Taverns," a town 32 miles (51 km) from Rome. A "tavern" was not a bar but a shop (Acts 28:15).

MACEDONIA

GREECE

Aegean Sea

GALATIA

CILICIA

PAMPHYLIA

SYRIA

Cnidus

Myra

RHODES

CRETE

CYPRUS

Cauda

Fair Haven

Mediterranean Sea

Sidon

Caesarea

Jerusalem

In Rome Paul has the freedom to teach about Jesus.
④

Come here, my little Max! Dr. Mo says, "You won't feel a thing!"

Let's make a deal! I pay you $999.99, and we become partners!

Ephesians

Paul

Paul wrote the letter to the Ephesians while he was sitting in prison in Rome. It is a beautiful letter that begins (after the usual greeting) with the longest sentence in the Bible. (The New International Version breaks it up into smaller sentences, but if you have a King James Version, you can see that it is really all one sentence.)

The sentence is that long because Paul was so excited about the wonderful things Jesus has done for us that he kept interrupting himself. Paul almost stumbled over his own words as he wrote this great song of praise – as he was sitting in prison!
Ephesians 1:3-14

In the first half of the letter Paul keeps talking about the wonderful things we have in Christ, and in the second half he kindly and gently tells us how we should live as Christians. Ephesians 4:25-32

He also talks to children and parents, and at the end of the letter he describes the "armor of God."
Ephesians 6:1-4
Ephesians 6:10-18

What's left of the great theater in Ephesus, where Paul was almost killed by an angry mob (see page 206). This is the last ruins picture – I promise!

Philippians

Paul

Paul wrote the letter to the Philippians also from jail in Rome. Being in jail is not exactly a reason to be happy, but in this letter Paul talks more about joy than in any other of his letters.

Paul's purpose in life was to preach about Jesus to anybody who wanted to listen – and even to those who did not want to listen. Paul could never have preached in Nero's palace in Rome – he would have been thrown out or, more likely, killed.

But God allowed Paul to be put in jail, and now Paul was happy because he had been able to talk about Jesus to some of the people in Nero's palace! And Paul's example helped other Christians in Rome to no longer be shy, but to talk about Jesus to others. *Philippians 1:12-14*

Paul wrote to the church in Philippi to say "thank you" for some money they had sent him to buy some of the necessities while he was in prison.

In a beautiful hymn, Paul tells us that we should imitate Jesus, who gave up everything to become not only a human being, but to die on the cross for our sake! *Philippians 2:5-11*

We should learn not to worry but to trust God. *Philippians 4:4-7*

And we should fill our minds with good things – not with trash! *Philippians 4:8-9*

How come Dr. Mo made things worse?

I don't know.

Maybe it was all those commands you typed in.

You know Dr. Mo is a bit like the law. In Romans 7 it says . . .

Deep, Jay. Real deep.

Colossians

Paul

In Colosse there were people who were teaching wrong things about Jesus, so Paul wrote to them to tell them again that Jesus Christ is the only way to salvation, and that what he has done for us is enough! *Colossians 1:15-23*

Paul also talks about what it means to live as a Christian. (By the way, being gentle and patient does not mean being a wimp! It means putting yourself in other peoples' shoes and treating them the way you would want to be treated.) *Colossians 3:12-14*

And toward the end of the letter he also talks about Christian relationships. *Colossians 3:18-4:1*

This letter to the church in Colosse and the letter to Paul's friend Philemon were taken to Colosse at the same time.

Read Romans 7:8-10!

Jay, why are they chasing us?

Philemon

Paul

This is a personal letter, written by Paul to his friend Philemon in Colosse. Philemon, who was a Christian, had a slave named Onesimus, who was not a Christian. One day Onesimus stole some things from Philemon and ran away, all the way to Rome, where Onesimus somehow met Paul in prison. Paul told him about Jesus, and Onesimus became a Christian.

Paul told Onesimus that he had to go back to Philemon. Onesimus was probably scared, because runaway slaves were often killed by their owners.

So Paul wrote this letter to ask Philemon to take Onesimus back – "no longer as a slave, but better than a slave, as a dear brother"! And Paul told Philemon that he himself would pay Philemon whatever Onesimus still owed him for the things he had stolen.

(By the way, "Onesimus" means "useful" – see if you can find Paul's plays on words.) *Philemon 1-25*

Dr. Mo says, "You **will** be our slaves!"

Hear that, kiddies?

Hurry! Just a few more books and we're out of the Bible!

They're going to crash my dad's computer!

The book of Acts ends right in the middle of the story of Paul, with Paul under house arrest. Luke was perhaps planning to write a third book, after the gospel of Luke and the book of Acts. It is too bad he didn't, because the third book might have told us how Paul was set free and how he made a fourth missionary journey, this time perhaps even farther west: to Spain. All we know about Paul from the time after he was released from prison we know from letters he wrote to his friends Timothy and Titus.

But after his fourth missionary journey Paul was put back into prison in Rome, this time in a real prison, actually more like a dungeon. And there he was put to death, about thirty years after he met Jesus on the road to Damascus and about two years before the Romans destroyed the temple in Jerusalem in A.D. 70.

1 and 2 Timothy

Paul

Paul thought very highly of Timothy, who was like a son to Paul.
🦋 *Philippians 2:19-22*

Timothy had traveled with Paul for a while, and now Timothy was the pastor of a young church. There were many things Timothy didn't know about being a pastor, and Paul wasn't going to be around to help him. So Paul wrote Timothy this letter to give him advice on things like what to do about people in the church who were causing problems, how to choose good elders and deacons, and how to take care of a large number of widows.

The most important thing Paul told Timothy about being a pastor was that he should set an example for the church by how he lived his own life. Paul wanted the Christians in Ephesus to look at Timothy and say, "Timothy may be young, but when I look at him I see how a Christian should live."

And Paul gave some excellent practical advice for everybody, for example, what to do if you have lots of money or things.
🦋 *1 Timothy 6:17-19*

When Paul wrote 1 Timothy he had been released from prison in Rome and was free to travel again. But only two years later, when he wrote 2 Timothy, things were very different. Emperor Nero had blamed the Christians for the fire that destroyed half of the city of Rome (which Nero may have set himself). Christians were arrested and executed left and right. Paul was also arrested and he was sent back to prison in Rome, this time on death row!

So when Paul wrote 2 Timothy he knew that it could be the very last letter he'd ever write. He tells Timothy that things are getting more and more difficult for Christians, but Timothy should keep on believing in Jesus and preaching the gospel – not what people want to hear, but the truth.
🦋 *2 Timothy 4:1-5*

Titus

Paul

Titus was in charge of several churches on the island of Crete, and Paul wrote the letter to Titus at the same time as the first letter to Timothy, while Paul was free again.

Paul tells Titus how to deal with people who create problems in the church. There were apparently people on Crete who were teaching false doctrine, and many people in the church listened to these false teachers. Titus had to learn how to stop these people.

And Paul talks to Titus about doing what is good. 🦋 *Titus 3:1-8*

1, 2, and 3 John

John

The apostle John probably wrote his three letters from Ephesus, where he was a pastor for many years. We don't know for sure when he wrote them, but it was probably when John was an old man, some twenty years after Peter and Paul died. John may have been the last of the apostles still alive.

His first letter is mostly about love and forgiveness. God is light, and we should live in God's light. One way to live in God's light is by loving others. ✤ 1 John 1:5-10 ✤ 1 John 2:7-11

And loving others is a very practical thing that is not just a feeling! ✤ 1 John 3:16-20

At the end, John makes it very clear what the message of the gospel is all about. God is love, and he showed his love by sending Jesus. ✤ 1 John 4:7-11 ✤ 1 John 5:10-12

The other two letters of the apostle John are very brief letters written to individuals in which he talks about being hospitable to Christians from other cities (it often wasn't easy to find a safe place to stay in a strange city).

Those guys sure ain't dragon their feet.

What is this? A horror movie?

No – we're in a vision from the book of Revelation!

Dr. Mo says, "MOMMY!"

Kiddies! Press the blitz button already!

The Roman writer Pliny was amazed that two Christians could show love to each other without ever having met before!

Revelation

The New Testament ends with a spectacular vision – and the promise that God will make all things new.

The apostle John had this vision while he was on Patmos, an island in the Mediterranean Sea, where he was exiled because he was a Christian. God gave John this vision to let Christians know that, no matter how bad things may get, in the end God will win.

When you read Revelation, you must always remember that it is a vision, something John saw. For example, in Revelation 12:3 you read about "an enormous red dragon with seven heads and ten horns and seven crowns on his heads. His tail swept a third of the stars from the sky and flung them to earth." The dragon is a picture of the enormous powers that will fight God and try to keep his plan from happening.

But what John talks about isn't just special effects! The suffering and pain are very real, and the people who suffer and die are real people.

The only way to get an idea of the book of Revelation is to read it. The first three chapters are letters from Jesus to seven churches in Asia Minor. Then begins the vision, in heaven.

Revelation 4:1-11

In God's right hand there is a scroll with writing, sealed with seven seals. The scroll contains God's plan to make all things new. But first, the seals must be broken so that the scroll can be opened and God's plan can be fulfilled. Only the Lion of the tribe of Judah, Jesus, can open the seals.

Revelation 5:1-13

The next thirteen chapters tell of all the terrible things that happen as the seals are broken. There are wars and illness and many people die. Sometimes it looks as if Satan will win.

This beautiful island is Patmos, where the apostle John had the most terrifying and wonderful vision anyone has ever had.

I've **got** it!

There's a file-protection program called Dr. Grace that will keep Mo and Max from destroying our program.

The Greek of Revelation is often very poor, perhaps because John was alone and did not have anyone to help him write good Greek.

But then, when all seven seals have been broken, John is back in heaven, where there is shouting and singing because the time has come for God to make all things new!
Revelation 19:5-8

Satan is finally defeated once and for all, and God creates a new heaven and a new earth. In the end, God will wipe away every tear from our eyes (the ones we cry and the tears inside us nobody can see), and there will be no more death or mourning or crying or pain!
Revelation 21:1-5

At the very end of Revelation Jesus says, "Yes, I am coming soon." And John's answer is, "Amen. Come, Lord Jesus!"

Some early Christians had difficulty accepting the book of Revelation as Scripture.

Way to go, Dr. Grace! Thanks!

You're welcome, Rebecca. Dr. Mo and Max can't get to you now — unless you let them. As long as you work together, you'll be fine.

I think we've lost them. But now where are we?

I don't know. I thought we'd be out of the program by now.

This place gives me the creeps.

Dr. Mo says, "Malpractice!"

Grace! I gotta deal for you, honey! Just listen!

The Church in Trouble

After the Bible

The total length of the corridors of the catacombs is said to be 500 miles. There are thirty-five known catacombs.

When the book of Revelation was written around A.D. 90 (that is, about 90 years after the birth of Christ), there were fewer churches in the whole world than you'll find today in one of the larger cities of North America. Most of those churches were in cities around the eastern part of the Mediterranean Sea, which all belonged to the Roman Empire.

It wasn't easy to be a Christian in those days. For more than 200 years the Roman emperors persecuted the church, in part because the Christians did not want to worship the emperor – they knew they should worship only God. Many Christians were killed, some in the Colosseum in Rome, a huge arena where Christians sometimes were brought to be killed by lions while thousands of people watched and cheered.

The only place where the Christians in the city of Rome could safely meet was the catacombs, which were large, underground hallways and rooms where people were buried. The Romans wouldn't go into the catacombs because there were dead bodies there, but the Christians weren't afraid, because they knew that Jesus had won over death.

Yet no matter how hard the Roman emperor tried to get rid of the church, more and more people became Christians and more and more churches were founded in the Roman Empire.

This is what a catacomb _really_ looks like.

Emperor Constantine

After the Bible

Then something totally unexpected happened: Around the year 300 the Roman Emperor Constantine became a Christian himself!

Now the church had a very different problem. Instead of persecuting Christians, Emperor Constantine wanted everyone to become a Christian. So, many people became Christians, not because they believed in Jesus but because they wanted to have a good job or live in a nice home.

And about 500 years after Emperor Constantine became a Christian, Emperor Charlemagne fought against pagan tribes in what is now Northern Europe and forced them to become Christians. Anyone who refused to become a Christian was killed. The Christians were now doing the persecuting! And the worst of it was that because everybody now was called a Christian, it was no longer clear who really believed in Jesus and who didn't.

An ancient wooden church in Heddal, Norway. Churches in other parts of the world can look very different.

The great cathedral in Rheims, France, was finished almost 800 years ago, during the time known as the Middle Ages or Dark Ages.

Three early Christian symbols were the good shepherd, the anchor (which stood for the cross), and the dove holding an olive branch (which stood for peace).

Are you a Christian?

Yes, I'm a Christian. Are you a Christian?

Yes, I'm a Christian. Are you a Christian? If not, we will kill you!

In that case, I'm a Christian!

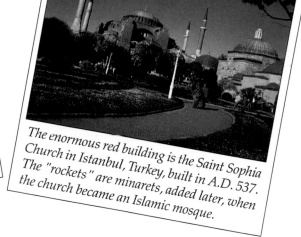

This is a more familiar kind of church for most of us. This little church stands in South Woodbury, Vermont.

The enormous red building is the Saint Sophia Church in Istanbul, Turkey, built in A.D. 537. The "rockets" are minarets, added later, when the church became an Islamic mosque.

But the church had still another problem. There were Christians who believed things about God and about Jesus that were different from what Jesus and the apostles had taught. So after Emperor Constantine became a Christian, all the churches met together several times to make clear once and for all what it was that all Christians should believe.

The church needed a brief, clear statement of the things all Christians should believe, that could easily be memorized. A statement like that is called a "creed." The best-known creed is the Apostles' Creed, which is read in many churches on Sunday.

The Apostles' Creed

What Does It Mean?

I believe in God

There is only one God. In the Bible we learn that he is three persons: the Father, the Son (Jesus), and the Holy Spirit.

the Father almighty, Creator of heaven and earth,

God the Father is almighty (all-powerful) – no one is more powerful than God. He made the whole universe by himself, out of nothing. And he made human beings special, to be like him.

and in Jesus Christ, his only Son,

When Adam and Eve lived in the Garden of Eden, they ate from the tree that God had told them not to eat from. Because they disobeyed God, all people are now sinners. We deserve to die because of our sins. But God sent his one and only Son, Jesus, into this world to save us from our sins.

our Lord.

When we say Jesus is our Lord, we say that he has the right to tell us what to do, and we promise to obey him.

He was conceived by the power of the Holy Spirit,

When Jesus was born into the world (we remember his birthday at Christmas), he did not have a human father, for God was his Father.

and born of the Virgin Mary.

But Jesus did have a human mother, Mary. She gave birth to Jesus just like any mother gives birth to a baby.

He suffered under Pontius Pilate,

Jesus taught many things about God and his kingdom, and he healed many people. But there were also many people who hated him for what he did and said. At last his enemies arrested him and put him on trial, even though he had never committed one sin in his entire life. Pontius Pilate, the Roman who was in charge of Palestine, allowed Jesus to be condemned to death.

was crucified,

Jesus died one of the most horrible kinds of death: death on a cross. He was crucified on Good Friday.

dead and buried. He descended to the dead.

Jesus really died and was buried in a grave. He died for our sins; that is, Jesus died in our place. We no longer need to be afraid to die.

On the third day he rose again.

On Easter Sunday, after being in the grave for three days, Jesus came to life again. He now lives forever. No one had ever done this before. Jesus proved that he was stronger than death and Satan.

He ascended into heaven,	Forty days after his resurrection, Jesus went back home to his Father in heaven.
and is seated at the right hand of the Father.	What is Jesus doing now in heaven? He is sitting on a throne, right next to God. He is in charge of everything that is happening in this world, and he is taking care of all of his people, including you and me!
He will come again to judge the living and the dead.	Someday Jesus will come back again to this earth. When this happens, all those who have ever believed on him will also rise again and go with him to heaven. All of his enemies will be cast into hell.
I believe in the Holy Spirit,	On Pentecost Sunday, Jesus sent his Spirit to the church. The Holy Spirit lives in us and helps us obey God and his Son Jesus.
the holy catholic church,	If we believe in Jesus, we belong to his church. Jesus wants us to tell others about him and so increase the size of his church. "Catholic" in the Apostles' Creed does not mean "Roman Catholic" but "universal" – the church of Jesus includes all Christians everywhere and whenever they have lived, live, or will live!
the communion of saints,	Christians everywhere should love and help each other, because we all are part of the same family.
the forgiveness of sins,	God was angry at us because we have all sinned. But because of his grace, he promises to forgive those sins if we ask Jesus to come into our hearts.
the resurrection of the body,	When we die, our bodies are laid in a grave, but we ourselves go to be with Jesus. And just as Jesus rose from the dead, someday those who believe in him will also rise from the dead and receive new, perfect bodies.
and the life everlasting.	When Jesus finally comes again and takes us to our home in heaven, he promises us that we will live forever and ever. We will never die again!
Amen.	"Amen" is a Hebrew word that means something like "Yes!" When you say "amen" at the end of a prayer, you say "Yes! I believe that you can do this, Lord." At the end of this creed it means, "Yes! This is what I believe!"

The Apostles' Creed was not written by the apostles, but it is a summary of what the apostles taught.

Nah! You guys come over here!

Because the sky and the ocean are blue I believe we should paint our churches blue!

But Jay I don't think it matters what color your Church is.

Amen!

The Church Divided

After the Bible

By the year 1000, the church split into two large groups who excommunicated each other – each one threw the other out of the church! The one group was headed by the bishop of Rome (the pope) and was therefore called the Roman Catholic Church. The other group was headed by the bishop of Constantinople (the patriarch) and is called the Eastern Orthodox Church because the churches in this group were all in the eastern part of Europe. (In many larger cities in the United States you'll find Greek Orthodox churches and Russian Orthodox churches, which are the two main groups in the Eastern Orthodox Church.)

In the Western church, the popes became more and more powerful. They almost became like kings. Some even had armies who could fight for them. Many were more interested in being rich than in following the teachings of Jesus and helping other people become good Christians. But we should remember that there were also many priests and monks who were concerned about people and tried to help them, especially the poor.

Meanwhile...

Look, the invisible wall is shattering! The kiddies have begun to fight!

Dr. Mo says, "Let's get them."

The beautiful cathedral of Saint Basil in Moscow. It was completed in 1554 and stands right next to the Kremlin.

I thought we believed in red?

Yes, red's right, but pink is perfect!

I think you should believe in a more royal shade of purple.

You think so?

I really think I prefer to believe in yellow.

I'll make a believer of you yet!

Bblllllbbxxxhhh.

Am I red enough for the red church?

But Dr. Grace told us not to fight. We're supposed to work together!

232

Around 1500 a very important change took place in the church. The pope began to teach that if people paid money to the church in Rome, their sins would be forgiven. A German monk named Martin Luther studied the Bible and discovered that the pope was wrong: God forgives our sins because of what Jesus has done for us – there is nothing we can do except say "thank you" to God. He began to write and preach about what he had found, and soon the pope threw him out of the church – but many people listened to Luther and so began the Protestant Reformation. (It is called "Protestant" because Luther and his followers were protesting against problems in the Roman Catholic Church.)

In the almost 500 years since the Reformation, the Protestant churches have been dividing into many different churches. There are Lutheran, Presbyterian, Baptist, Episcopal, Methodist, Pentecostal, and many other churches – sometimes across the street from each other.

In the early church, when Christians were persecuted, it was obvious who was a Christian and who was not. But after Emperor Constantine became a Christian, almost everybody became a Christian, and just because a person belonged to a church didn't mean that that person really believed in Jesus. When we stand before God's throne he won't ask us which church we belonged to, but whether we believed in his Son!

This adobe church in Taos Pueblo, New Mexico, shows how even within a single country people can express their faith differently (compare it with the white church on page 229).

What Is the Bible?

The Bible is the book that tells us
- Who God is
- What God is like
- What God has done, is doing, and will do
- What we should do.

But the Bible isn't just about God, it is also from God. The Bible is God's Word. It tells us everything we need to know to be right with God (to be saved) and to please God. The apostle Paul says that Scripture (another name for the Bible) is inspired and useful for teaching us what is true, to make us understand what is wrong in our lives, to straighten us out, and to help us do what is right (2 Timothy 3:16 - 17).

God could have given us a book of theology that only really smart and educated people could understand. Or he could have given us a book of rules that told us what to do and what not to do.

Instead, God gave us a book with many different things: stories, poems, letters, laws, proverbs, and lots of other things. No one will ever completely know and understand everything that is in the Bible. But everybody can understand stories, and everybody can understand that God tells us in the Bible that he loves us very much.

God took more than 1,500 years to write the Bible, and he used more than forty different people. Some of those people were rich, some were poor. Among them were kings, poets, prophets, musicians, philosophers, farmers, teachers, a priest, a statesman, a sheep herder, a tax collector, a medical doctor, and a couple of fishermen. They wrote the Bible on three continents: Asia, Europe, and Africa, in palaces and in prisons, in cities and in the wilderness, in times of war and in times of peace.

DR. GRACE! WE'RE SORRY! HELP US!

And what about our evil viruses, Max and his hideous henchman, Dr. Mo? Will the forces of darkness triumph over Grace?

Is this the end of our daring adventurers? Separated by petty differences, unable to move ahead . . . will they be able to escape their gloomy fate?

The first American Bible was printed in Boston in 1752.

How Did We Get Our Bible?

The Bible was written long before paper was invented. The earliest books of the Bible were written on flat tablets of clay or on dried, scraped animal skins (called "parchment") or perhaps on sheets of papyrus, made of the grass-like papyrus plant. Those skins or papyrus leaves were glued together to make a long roll or scroll.

The Bible was written several thousand years before the printing press was invented, so for thousands of years the books of the Bible were copied by hand, over and over again. Of course, very few people could afford to have their own Bible.

That didn't change until Johann Gutenberg invented the printing press around 1450. One of the first books to be printed was the Bible, and more and more people now could afford their own Bible.

But then there was another problem. Most people couldn't read the Bible in the languages in which it was written (Hebrew, Aramaic, and Greek), so the Bible had to be translated into languages people could understand.

This was already true before the time of Jesus. The Bible of the Jews (our Old Testament) was written mostly in Hebrew, and many Jews, especially those who lived outside of Palestine, had forgotten their Hebrew; they spoke mostly Greek. So the Old Testament was first translated into Greek about 200 years before the time of Jesus. That translation is called the Septuagint.

Then, after the time of Jesus, when the church spread through the Roman Empire, the Bible was translated into Latin, because that was what people spoke.

When the printing press was invented, only scholars still knew Latin, so the Bible had to be translated into languages people spoke: German, French, English, and so on, so the average people could read the Bible for themselves.

The best-known English version (another name for translation) is the King James Version, which was published in 1611. It is a beautiful translation, but the English language has changed somewhat since 1611, so that it is sometimes difficult to understand (try James 1:21 in the King James Version!).

Today there are many translations in modern English. The best-known are the New International Version (NIV), which was published in 1978, and the Living Bible (1971).

The Egyptian bishop Athanasius of Alexandria in A.D. 367 was the first person to list the twenty-seven New Testament books we now have.

And what about Chip's father's multimillion dollar computer system? Is this the end of the program, the crashing of the computer empire, the halting of holography?

Tune in next page, same time, same book, to see if our holographic heroes will overcome!

235

The Jewish Bible

The Jewish Bible (the Bible Jesus used) is our Old Testament. The first five books (Genesis, Exodus, Leviticus, Numbers, Deuteronomy) are considered the most important part; together they are called the Law, or, in Hebrew, the Torah. In synagogues today the scroll on which the Torah is written is kept in a special case, called the ark, that stands in the place of honor. The other sections in the Hebrew Bible are called the Prophets and the Writings. The Jews looked after the Word of God for many centuries, which is why we have our Old Testament today!

Thomas Jefferson published an edition of the New Testament that left out everything supernatural, such as the miracles, because he did not believe they happened.

Ah, they're working together again. Now I can help them!

This is a job for . . .

SUPER FROGGO

Andrew Jackson said of the Bible, "That book is the rock on which our republic rests."

The Canon of the Bible

The sixty-six books of our Bible are also called the canon of the Bible. Those sixty-six books, from Genesis to Revelation, are the only ones that are part of the inspired Word of God. Most of the people who wrote those books didn't know that their writings would become part of the Bible, but the church recognized that they were special. Jesus quoted from the Jewish Bible, our Old Testament, and made it clear that it was the Word of God. The church recognized that some of the writings of the apostles and people who worked with the apostles (for example, Luke) were special – they were inspired and should be part of the canon.

The Apocrypha

Some Bibles have more than sixty-six books. Those extra books are called the Apocrypha. They are books the church never accepted as part of the canon but that some churches wanted to keep with the Bible because they were worthwhile. Included in the Apocrypha are the books of the Maccabees that tell about the time between the Old and New Testaments.

Foiled again!

Who do you think Max represents? See Genesis 3 and Romans 7-8.

One of the most important Greek manuscripts of the New Testament, called the Codex Sinaiticus, was discovered at St. Catherine's monastery at the foot of Mount Sinai, in the 1800s.

The Dead Sea Scrolls

Along the shore of the Dead Sea are steep cliffs dotted with caves high off the ground. Nobody paid much attention to them until in 1947 a large number of pottery jars were found in one of those caves. In those jars were scrolls, ancient books that had been written around the time of Jesus. Those "Dead Sea Scrolls" had been hidden in the caves by a religious Jewish group when the Romans came and destroyed Jerusalem in A.D. 70. One of the scrolls was a copy of Isaiah that was several hundred years older than any copy of Isaiah that was known to exist in 1947! The amazing thing is that the text of the Dead Sea scroll of Isaiah is virtually identical to the text we have. God has kept his Word from being changed in the process of copying it for so many centuries.

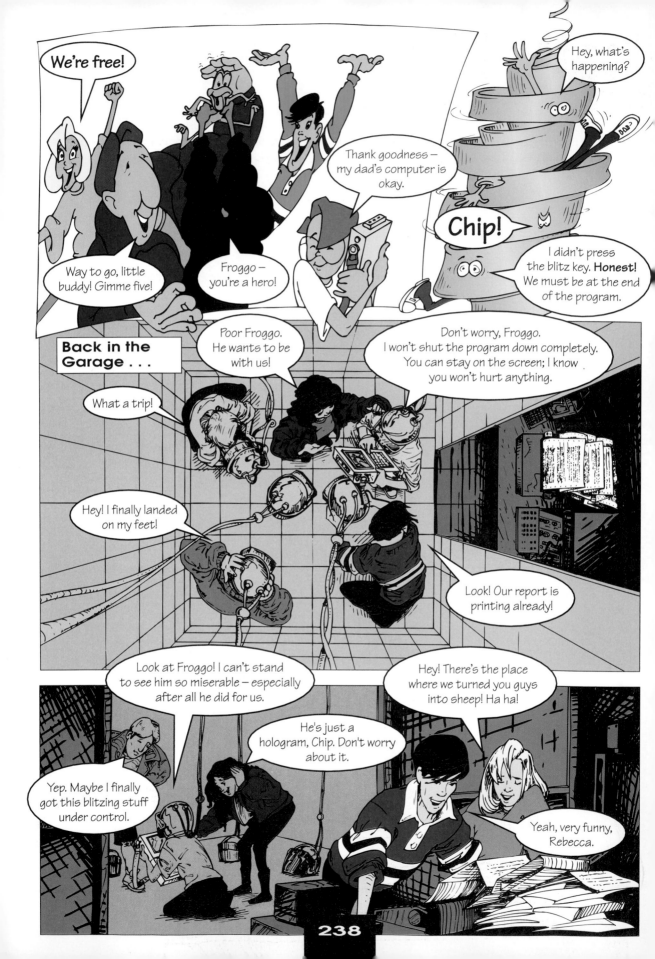

Reading Guide

These are the parts of the Bible where we got most of our information for Professor Ed (who calls them "sources"). Besides, we wanted to give you a chance to read all these great stories for yourself – or with your whole family.

So grab your Bible and start reading. And don't worry that you don't have holographic reality – your imagination works just as well.

Here are some hints for the Bible readings in case you're confused:

- Most of the readings are the same ones we put in our report.
- Not all readings are the same length (some will take you only a couple of minutes, others will take you longer).
- You can check off the reading when you're finished (it'll give you a great feeling of accomplishment!).
- You'll find that not all readings are in the same order as they are in the Bible. For example, you'll find the book of Proverbs in the middle of readings from 1 Kings. That's because the readings are in historical order, and Proverbs was written (in large part at least) by King Soloman, whose story is found in 1 Kings. To make things less confusing, we've put readings that are not in their usual biblical place in grey boxes. (See pages 130 and 131 for a better explanation.)
- Read the pages in our report along with the Bible readings – you'll learn so much fun stuff your head will burst!

Jay

Old Testament

Moses (How the Israelites got out of Egypt) (Pages 36-39)

From Egypt into the wilderness (Pages 40-42)

God gives the Law at Sinai (Page 43-44, 48)

The golden calf (Pages 45-46)

The tabernacle (Page 46-47)

The twelve spies; forty more years in the wilderness (Pages 49-52)

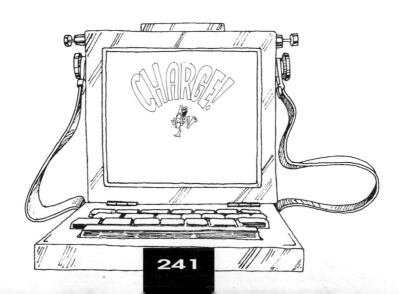

Moses' week-long farewell sermon (Page 54)

- ❑ When Moses dies, Joshua will take his place
- ❑ Love the Lord!
- ❑ Get rid of all the nations who now live in Canaan
- ❑ Moses dies

Numbers 27:12-23
Deuteronomy 6:1-25
Deuteronomy 7:1-16
Deuteronomy 34:1-12

The Israelites finally move into Canaan (Pages 55- 59)

- ❑ Rahab and the Israelite spies
- ❑ Israel finally goes across the Jordan River
- ❑ Joshua and the battle of Jericho
- ❑ Why the Israelites were defeated at Ai
- ❑ The day the sun stood still
- ❑ Joshua says good-bye

Joshua 2:1-24
Joshua 3:1-17
Joshua 6:1-27
Joshua 7-8
Joshua 10:1-15
Joshua 24:28-33

The sad time of the Judges (Pages 60-65)

- ❑ Disobedience and defeat
- ❑ The gross story of Ehud, the left-handed judge
- ❑ Deborah, the woman who became judge
- ❑ Gideon, the judge who scared a whole army
- ❑ Samson, the judge who got a haircut

Judges 2:6-3:4; 21:25
Judges 3:12-30
Judges 4:1-24
Judges 6:1-7:24
Judges 13:1-16:31

The story of Ruth (Pages 66-67)

- ❑ A story of loyalty, honesty, and love

Ruth 1-4

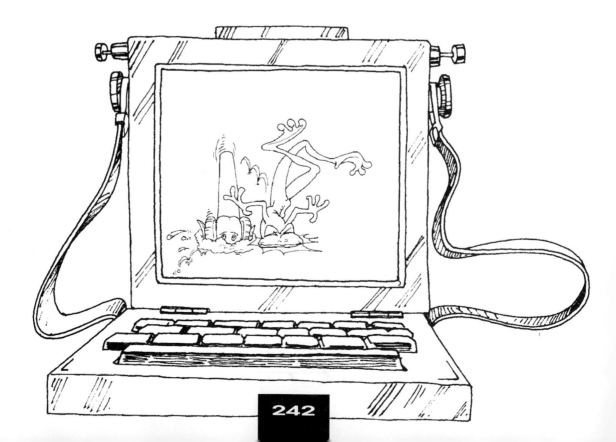

Samuel, the last Judge (Pages 68-71)

❏ Samuel is born and goes to live at the tabernacle	1 Samuel 1:1-28
❏ God calls Samuel in the middle of the night	1 Samuel 3:1-21
❏ The Israelites use the ark as their mascot – and the Philistines take it	1 Samuel 4:1-11
❏ God convinces the Philistines to return the ark	1 Samuel 5:1-12; 6:10-12; 6:21-7:1
❏ The Philistines are scared of thunder	1 Samuel 7:7-11

Saul, the first king of Israel (Pages 72-73)

❏ The Israelites want a king	1 Samuel 8:1-22
❏ Saul loses some donkeys and ends up being anointed king	1 Samuel 9:1-10:1; 10:17-27
❏ The king who hid among the luggage	1 Samuel 10:17-27
❏ The king who tried to cheat God	1 Samuel 15:1-34

David and Saul (Pages 74-80)

❏ Samuel anoints David to be the new king	1 Samuel 16:1-13
❏ David becomes Saul's court musician	1 Samuel 16:14-23
❏ David beats Goliath, the Philistine bully	1 Samuel 17:1-58
❏ Saul figures out that David will be the next king	1 Samuel 18:1-16
❏ David and Jonathan – the story of great friendship	1 Samuel 20:1-42
❏ David has a chance to kill Saul	1 Samuel 24:1-22
❏ Saul and the witch of Endor	1 Samuel 28:1-25
❏ Saul kills himself	1 Samuel 31:1-5

The story of Job (Page 79)

❏ How Job ended up on the dump	Job 1:1-2:13
❏ Job gets mad at his friends	Job 12:2-3; 16:2-5; 19:2-3
❏ Job cries for somebody to speak to God on his behalf – but he still trusts God	Job 9:32-33; 19:25
❏ God tells Job that Job isn't as smart as he thinks he is	Job 38:1-21
❏ The happy ending	Job 42:1-16

David finally becomes king (Pages 80-87)

❏ David finally becomes king	2 Samuel 5:1-12
❏ The ark of the covenant is brought to Jerusalem	2 Samuel 6:1-23
❏ God's wonderful promises to David	2 Samuel 7:11b-16
❏ An example of David's song writing	2 Samuel 22:1-20; Psalm 18:1-19
❏ David's sin with Bathsheba	2 Samuel 11:1-27
❏ David asks God for forgiveness	2 Samuel 12:1-14
❏ David's prayer for forgiveness	Psalm 51
❏ The story of Absalom	2 Samuel 18:5-17; 19:4

Psalms – the songbook of God's people (Pages 82-83)

❏ The great song about God's goodness	Psalm 23
❏ A psalm to pray when you are sorry	Psalm 32
❏ A psalm for when you are thankful	Psalm 100
❏ A psalm to praise God with	Psalm 103
❏ A psalm for when you are sad	Psalm 130

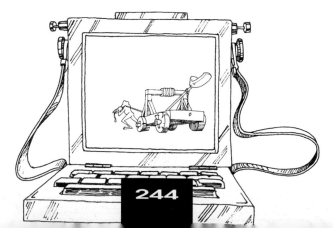

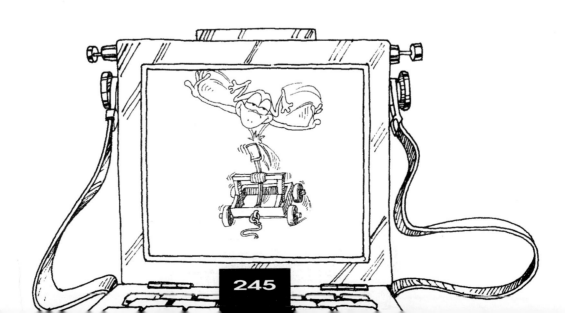

New Testament

It will help if you read pages 132 through 141 before you begin reading in the New Testament. They explain all the things that happened between the end of the Old Testament and the beginning of the New Testament.

John the Baptist is born (Page 144)

Jesus is born (Pages 145-146)

Jesus' youth (Pages 146-147)

Jesus and John the Baptist (Pages 148-149)

Jesus begins to preach and teach (Pages 150-153)

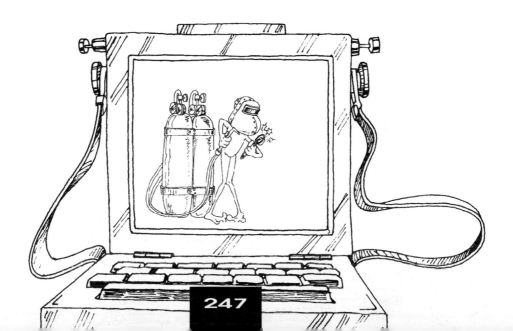

Some parables Jesus told (Pages 154-155)

❏ The good Samaritan	Luke 10:30-37
❏ The lost (prodigal) son	Luke 15:11-32
❏ The rich man and Lazarus	Luke 16:19-31
❏ The wise and the foolish builder	Matthew 7:24-27
❏ The sower and the seed	Mark 4:3-8, 14-20
❏ The lost sheep	Luke 15:4-7
❏ The talents	Luke 19:12-27
❏ The parable of the weeds	Matthew 13:24-30

Some of the miracles Jesus performed (Pages 158-161)

❏ Water into wine	John 2:1-11
❏ Jesus brings a young man back to life	Luke 7:11-16
❏ The faith of the centurion	Luke 7:1-10
❏ Jesus calms the storm	Mark 4:35-41
❏ A dead girl and a sick woman	Mark 5:21-43
❏ Jesus feeds the five thousand	Mark 6:32-44
❏ Jesus walks on the water	Matthew 14:22-33
❏ Jesus heals the man born blind	John 9:1-34
❏ The coin in the fish	Matthew 17:24-27
❏ Ten lepers are healed, but only one says "thank you"	Luke 17:11-19
❏ The miraculous catch of fish	Luke 5:1-11
❏ The lame man who couldn't make it to the pool	John 5:1-15
❏ The evil spirits and the pigs	Matthew 8:28-34
❏ Jesus heals on the Sabbath	Matthew 12:9-14
❏ Jesus raises Lazarus from the dead	John 11:1-46

Some of the things Jesus taught (Page 162)

❏ The Beatitudes	Matthew 5:1-12
❏ The Sermon on the Mount	Matthew 5:33-48
❏ The Sermon on the Mount: Giving and praying	Matthew 6:1-15
❏ The Sermon on the Mount: Where is your treasure?	Matthew 6:19-24
❏ The Sermon on the Mount: Do not worry	Matthew 6:25-34
❏ The Sermon on the Mount	Matthew 7:1-29
❏ Rest for the weary	Matthew 11:25-30
❏ The greatest commandment	Mark 12:28-34
❏ Prayer	Luke 11:1-13

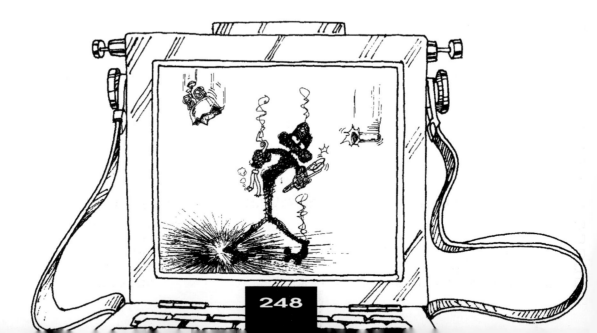

Some other events of Jesus' ministry (Page 163)

Jesus and the Pharisees (Pages 164-169)

The Last Supper (Pages 170-171)

In the Garden of Gethsemane (Page 172)

Jesus' trial before the Jewish Sanhedrin (Pages 173-175)

Jesus' trial before the Roman governor, Pontius Pilate (Page 176)

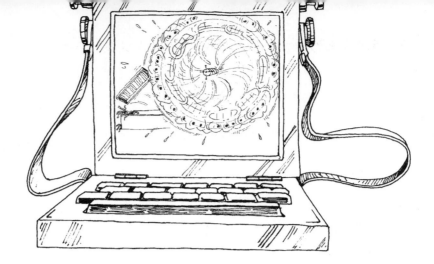

Index

Look on page 4 if you want to find a book of the Bible.

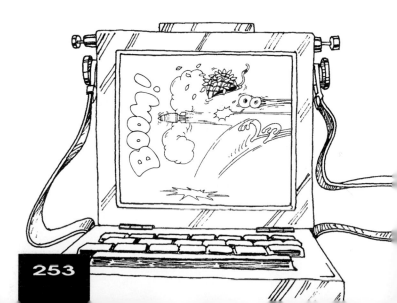

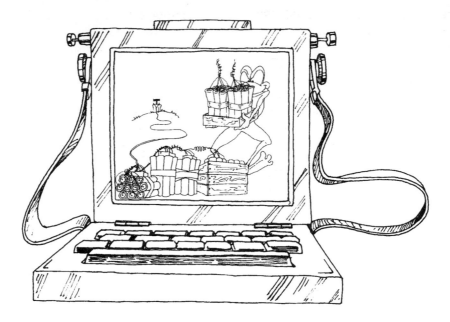

Fun Quiz

- What is the longest verse in the Bible?
- Why did the Midianites use camels in battle instead of horses?
- Why is there a green giant in this book?
- On what page does Max show up for the first time?
- On what page does Abraham Lincoln appear?
- What two pages in the book are missing?
- How many times does Brad land on his head in this book?

- What page in this book tells you how to be accepted by God?
- How many times does Froggo show up in this book?

Send your name, address and answers to:

"Fun Quiz"
P.O. Box 160, Maple Ridge, BC Canada
V2X 7G1

Correct entries are eligible for one of 50 wonderful prizes!

Photo Credits:

Valentino Almendarez & Karl VanRoon: 92
Art Resource: 178–79
V. Gilbert Beers: 26, 57, 144A-B, 177, 186, 188, 213A-D, 217, 220, 226, 227
Seffi Ben-Yosef: 32
Ben Chapman: 24, 42-43, 44-45, 61, 78, 89, 94, 119, 126, 137, 138-39, 143, 149, 156, 163, 180, 197, 204, 209, 215
FourByFive: 32-33
Sonia Halliday: 217

R. & E. Hecht Museum, Haifa University: 169
William LaSor: 21
Erich Lessing: 62, 173
Zev Radovan: 30, 35, 36B, 37, 50, 51A-D, 55, 70, 74, 100, 103, 115, 117, 136, 193
Tony Stone Images: Front cover
Superstock: 31, 41, 109, 148, 170–71, 172, 181, 228, 229A-B, 230, 231